The
Worcestershire
Village Book

THE VILLAGES OF BRITAIN SERIES

Other counties in this series include

The Worcestershire Village Book

Compiled by the Worcestershire
Federation of Women's Institutes from notes
and illustrations sent by Institutes in the County

Published jointly by
Countryside Books, Newbury
and the WFWI, Worcester

First published 1988
Reprinted 1989

Countryside Books
3 Catherine Road
Newbury, Berkshire

Cover photograph of Severn Stoke
by courtesy of the Heart of England Tourist Board

Produced through MRM Associates, Reading
Typeset by Acorn Bookwork, Salisbury
Printed in England by J. W. Arrowsmith Ltd., Bristol

Foreword

The lovely county of Worcestershire covers over 700 square miles and has at its heart the majestic cathedral City of Worcester.

The hills of the county form a natural barrier from the adjacent counties, the Malverns to the west, Bredon Hill to the south and the Clent and Lickeys to the north. The county is well known for its beautiful villages, some of them with black and white timber framed houses, others in the area around Broadway of mellow Cotswold stone.

Visitors are attracted to Worcestershire for the fruit and vegetables from the lush orchards of the Vale of Evesham and for the beautiful Worcester Porcelain.

Many famous people have lived in the county and have left their mark, among them Sir Edward Elgar who is the inspiration for a delightful scenic route through parts of the county, A. E. Housman and Jenny Lind the 'Swedish Nightingale'.

The members of the village W.I.s have enjoyed researching their village history. Their enthusiasm and interest for this book we hope, will encourage many to come and see for themselves the joy and beauty of Worcestershire.

Pat Harris
County Chairman

Acknowledgements

The Worcestershire Federation of Women's Institutes wish to thank all Institutes whose members worked hard to provide information and drawings for their villages including the Bredon Hill villages, and the following who provided additional material: Mr Dew (Eldersfield), Catherine Kealy (county map), and Barbara Edwards (map decoration). Finally, a special thank you to the co-ordinator of the project Betty Hudson and the county secretary Brenda Spragg and her assistant Greta Lawrie for their help.

The County of Worcestershire

Abberley Village

Abberley 🌿

Abberley Village, Abberley Common, Abberley Hill – to the stranger, three separate villages. The Ordnance Survey map however, shows the common and the village nestling round the foot of the hill while dwellings on the hill complete the circle.

It is a village with two churches, farms, cottages, black and white architecture among the red-brick new housing developments and modern conversions of old property. There is a village shop, petrol garage, and two repair shops, a school, village hall, cricket club and The Manor Arms which once brewed its own ale.

Victorian estate cottages are evidence that the occupants of Abberley Hall, now a preparatory school, were once landowners of most of the village, together with The Elms, today a hotel.

The main road from Worcester rises to a point on the saddle of the hill before descending into the village. Before 1760 an earlier road passed the historic spot nearby, marked by an oak tree, where St Augustine in 603 is reported by the Venerable Bede to have met the Welsh Bishops.

Old St Michael's church is still in use. A Norman church built about 1160 on a Saxon site, it is now part-ruin with the chancel restored – a favourite for christenings. It was here during restoration of the walls in the early 1960s that the famous 12th century silver spoons were found, now in the British Museum, while repairs to the vault disclosed leather fish-tail shaped coffins. The ghost of the 'Grey Lady' is said to haunt the church and nearby Rectory.

During the 1840s St Michael's was in such disrepair that a new church, St Mary's was built. It was dedicated in 1852. The day after, the tower of old St Michael's fell to the ground. New St Mary's was accidently burnt down in 1873, reputedly by a choir-boy trying to dry out the organ, and was finally rebuilt in 1877.

In about 1870 Joseph Jones, whose family fortunes were founded on the Manchester cotton industry, came to live at the Hall. It was his great interest in new methods of agriculture that gave the village much of its present shape. In 1884 he built the Clocktower, a familiar landmark, as a memorial to his wife – though some say as a time-keeper for his farm workers!

Coal had been supplied to Worcester during the 13th and 14th centuries and several drift mines were owned by the estate but later abandoned because of flooding. This coal was converted into coke for

9

hop-drying. Lime kilns operated from the 1700s. There were saw mills and the village had its own brickworks and kilns, using local clay. Two quarries supplied the villages with stone; one is still in commercial use today.

The present school, built in 1859 by the church is on the site of a charity school founded in 1717 by Elizabeth, widow of Joseph Walsh. An extra classroom was built in the 1880s to cater for the growing population with 118 children. Today, 40 children attend this parochial school before going on to Martley at the age of 11.

The population dwindled and 30 years ago there were only two babies in the village. In the late 1960s council houses were built, and then private housing estates and many cottage conversions. Today Abberley has approximately the same population as 100 years ago which occupies almost twice the number of houses.

Abberton ✍

A hamlet on a hill, once Eabba's settlement. There are about 20 houses, no new buildings, but a very extensive farm. The church of St Eadburga is 19th century but contains a Late Norman round font. The spire of the church was removed at the request of the RAF as it presented a hazard to aircraft using the airfield at Pershore.

Abbots Morton ✍

A pastoral village, well away from towns and main roads. The village street has many splendid examples of black and white cottages and houses, and there are two working farms in the centre of the village. A post office marks the end of the village to the east, and the church is at the west end. St Peter's is of Saxon origin, but rebuilt in the 12th century by the Normans.

The village hall is a First World War army hut, restored in 1925 with donations of 2/6d to cover cost. Ecclesiastical connections with the monks of Evesham explain the name of the village.

Alfrick ✒

Alfrick is set in beautiful mixed farming country with a pleasant undulating character, skirted to the north by the river Teme and close to Leigh brook which joins it near Leigh Court.

The village's ancient origins are implicit in its place name although there is a difference of opinion about this. The *Oxford Dictionary of Place Names* tells us that its most ancient form is 'Ealdred's Wic' and that this means that it was once the home of a prominent Saxon dairy farmer and named after him. A little later, the name appears as Alferwyke and Alfredeswic and in the 15th and 16th centuries, various versions of the name appear in documents, including the modern form – Alfrick.

Yet another fascinating theory is that the name means 'elf' or 'fairy kingdom' (elf-reich) and this perhaps ties up with the village's recent designation by a local paper as 'the most haunted village in Worcestershire'. There are many stories told of haunted places in and around Alfrick and of the ghosts of a black greyhound-like dog, a man and a horse, a wagon drawn by four black horses, a strange crow and various unearthly noises heard at night such as the persistent sound of a cooper's hammer. An older resident also tells of a man and woman who, with their dog, are to be seen walking from the old forge in the centre of the village, formerly operated by a Mr Leach, to the 13th century church of St Mary Magdalene, situated on a green knoll.

This beautiful little church could justly form the subject of an article all to itself. Perhaps its chief claim to fame lies in the fact that its one-time incumbent was the Reverend Dodgson, brother of Lewis Carroll who visited Alfrick frequently, staying at Upper House, then the rectory, and preaching in the church. Another literary connection with Alfrick was a Mrs Holland who lived at Alfrick Court and was the mother of Mrs Gaskell, author of *Cranford*.

Alfrick in the 1980s, however, seems for the most part far removed from such legends and stories of times past . . . and long past! Changes have not always been for the better. For instance, the children of the village received an education here 200 years ago and in 1884, Alfrick primary school opened, carrying on the good work for 100 years, to be unfortunately closed in 1984, thus ending a tradition. The Victorian buildings are now undergoing conversion. Once Alfrick boasted two public-houses, the Swan and the Wobbly Wheel but the latter is now a private house and only the Swan remains. At one time there was a butcher's shop, a village bakery, a milkman, a basket maker and a blacksmith. Today's villagers are still well served by a modern shop and post office, always busy.

Much residential development has taken place, transforming the centre of the village. There are many modern houses and bungalows and a small council estate. Social events take place in the 'new' village hall, opened in 1953 as a result of fund-raising by local people and replacing the former hall on the opposite side of the road. An Old Time Dancing Club ran regular dances there but even before this, young people and children used to enjoy Saturday night entertainment down at Bridge's Stone, in the shape of film shows and music from Mr Bill Costello's pianola. He produced his own electricity with the aid of a water-wheel in Leigh brook, long before electricity came to the village in 1949–50. Ten years later the water services arrived, and the village as it is today was born.

Alvechurch ✒

Although on high ground, Alvechurch is in a hollow, surrounded by hills. New views of the area have recently been opened up by the building of the M42 motorway which cuts across north-east Worcestershire, whilst still leaving most of the old charm and character of the village untouched.

Alvechurch derives its name from a Christian woman named Aelfgyth, who in AD780 founded a church on the site where the parish church of St Laurence stands today, with its Norman tower and combination of Anglo-Saxon building and extensive Victorian restoration. A stained glass window commemorates the Coronation of the young Queen Victoria in 1837. A tomb of a knight of the 1189 Crusade is also in the church.

Alvechurch has a wide range of architectural styles with many good examples of the Worcestershire type of half-timbered 16th century 'Hall Houses', red-brick cottages and recent modern development.

In 1361 the scourge of the Middle Ages, the bubonic plague, struck Alvechurch. Local inhabitants who died were buried in a communal pit and Pestilence Lane was so named because it lead to this pit.

Original mills of the area still remain. The Bishop's mill for milling grain, is now Mill Farm in Radford Road and in Rectory Lane there was a polishing mill serving the needle industry of Redditch. The river Arrow, which flows through the village, provided the power for these mills. A brick-yard and a tannery (hence Tanyard Lane) were the major industries

12

The Square, Alvechurch

of the area in the early 20th century. In recent times, engineering work has become the most prominent industry.

Considerable social activity has always been evident in the village and there are several active Societies with enthusiastic local support. Alvechurch also boasts cricket and football teams, Brownie and Guide Companies, church-based Youth Clubs and Women's Fellowships, branches of the Royal British Legion, Toc'H' and University of the Third Age. Two play-groups, modern schools, the 'Mayflower' Club for the over-60's and a library satisfy all ages and tastes.

In the centre of the village stands the attractive village hall erected in 1927 on land, and with money, bequeathed, and augmented by donations from parishioners. The Baptist church founded in 1826, also has a modern hall built with money raised by the local community. Both of these halls prove popular venues for exhibitions, social events and meetings.

Alvechurch has three public houses – the modern Red Lion, The White Swan and the Crown Inn at Withybed Green in a picturesque setting near the Worcester-Birmingham Canal. There are also two popular Social Clubs, with similar amenities, at both the cricket and football grounds and also at the canal-side Boating Marina.

In Alvechurch, once a borough with a mayor, the 'Beating of the

Bounds' is carried out periodically by local residents, establishing the boundary of the parish. The annual 'Mop Fair' originating in King John's days, continues to be held in early October, though on a much diminished scale. Carnivals, torch-light processions and bonfires with fireworks were at one time also held, but such events have now ceased, and there remains only the annual Summer Church Garden Fete.

Alvechurch provides practically every amenity and facility within a caring community, with its residents of varied careers, talents and crafts enriching village life.

Areley Kings 🦢

Once there was nothing but forest along the Severn's banks, but Ernleye, meaning 'eagles' clearing' eventually became the parish of Areley. A Norman church was built on a bank overlooking the Severn and about the year 1200, Layamon lived here as the earliest recorded priest of the parish. He was the author of *Brut*, one of the first poems in the English language. The parish, part of the Royal Manor of Martley, was entitled to add Kings to its name.

Monks had a fishery at Ernleye but after the Dissolution of the Monasteries the land passed to the Lord of the Manor, Simon Mucklow, who built Areley Hall and whose descendants still live there. The Mucklow family were Royalists and Prince Rupert slept at Areley Hall around the time of the Battle of Worcester.

Redstone Lane and the Rough were sandy tracks leading to the ford or 'passage' at Redstone. Near the sandstone caves, once a hermitage and later occupied by villagers, was an old coaching house which accommodated passengers waiting to ford the river. This house has now disappeared. It is said that the body of Prince Arthur was taken this way to cross the river on its way from Ludlow to Worcester Cathedral for burial in April 1502. Another building of interest in Redstone Lane was the old workhouse, later converted into four dwelling houses, now demolished to make way for modern bungalows.

James Brindley brought the Staffordshire & Worcestershire Canal to the Severn in 1770 and the new town of Stourport grew up around this important waterway junction. The Severn toll bridge was built in 1774, but across the water on what is still called 'The Christian Shore' the village remained a scattered community of farms and cottages.

In 1779, on the edge of the high common land, John Zachary of Areley

Hall, built a redbrick tower windmill four storeys high with a boat cap, four sails and a long tail pole. In those days, the mill and miller's cottage below and one or two tiny cottages were the only buildings along Areley Common, but following the Land Enclosures Act of 1844, small portions of land were awarded to various landowners and from about 1860 onward, a rash of typically Victorian cottages grew along the old drift road, still called Areley Common. After an active life of around 100 years, new steam-driven mills had made the windmill redundant and its sails and cap gradually decayed but around the beginning of this century, the Rector, Daniel Vawdrey, had it converted to a house.

The present Severn bridge, built in 1870, was originally a toll bridge. At last the day came, 3rd April 1893, when the toll was to be removed. Many people who had faithfully paid their tolls over the years gathered, wondering who would be the first to cross the bridge free. The honour fell upon a little old lady of 75, Mrs Jane Lane, quite a character in the village. Seated proudly in her donkey cart, she was escorted over the bridge between the waiting crowds and made a triumphant passage through the town.

The village of Areley Kings has grown enormously. Residential building commenced on the Walshes Farm land about 1946 and now the estate is so large that a First and Middle School, the Old Farm Inn, a parade of shops and a Tenants' Hall have all been built.

Areley Court and the glebe land near the church have been developed. The old black and white timber-framed Church House has recently been restored and is now a popular venue for social occasions. Dunley Park was built in the late 1960s and in the 1980s there has been further development at Astley Cross.

This has made Areley Common very busy with private cars and regular bus services, but fortunately, there is a ban on lorries except for access, so the huge trucks loaded with sugar beet ply around the perimeter of the village. Business people commute to Birmingham and there is work in the carpet factories and industrial estates between Stourport and Kidderminster.

The Parish Room is a hive of activity used by the majority of local organisations. The Recreation Ground houses the new Scout Hut and once a year the fair is staged on the field. On the first Saturday in September the Stourport Carnival Parade assembles there to be judged before wending its way to town.

Ashton Under Hill

Ashton Under Hill is a highly sought after, even modish place to live. Charm of location and buildings answer 20th century nostalgia, but equally attractive is its quiet location, close to major routes but away from the modern curse of high volume through traffic. Agriculture and horticulture has greatly diminished, but it still gives an attractive rural image to the area.

A thriving village school of over 60 pupils and several daily bus services to local towns help to attract and hold a population of wide age range.

The sub-post office at Ashton under Hill is contained in an old thatched cottage that is about 400 years old. It has had several uses including a shoe repair business. All the ceilings are beamed and very low and the rooms are very small. The post office is kept very busy at a time when many others are being forced to close.

Villagers are kept up to date about local events by consulting the special calendar there. The post office has been run by the Whitehead family for over 40 years, the present postmaster being the son, and it continues to be an essential 'gossip' shop for the village!

Most of the older part of the village is a conservation area. There are 17 listed buildings including an 18th century Georgian house and others of great merit and interest. Outside the parish church, with its Norman south door and embattled tower, is a 14th century stone cross with a three step base, a shaft and sundial. Across the road is an ancient cowshed with a line of rare connecting stone drinking troughs. This building used to be in the grounds of Middle Farm, itself a listed building of rubble and tile, but it was sold together with an adjacent old barn.

There are early black and white thatched cottages with delightful gardens, one of which used to be the Old Plough public house. Another listed building is the Manor House.

The area is dominated by the south eastern side of the unique Cotswolds outcrop known as Bredon Hill. Predominantly rural, the lower slopes of the hill are under cultivation, whilst the steeper grades offer grazing for sheep and cows together with cover for various forms of wildlife.

There are wonderful views over the vale of Evesham to the Lickeys in the north, the Cotswolds in the east and the Severn Valley to the south. The Wychavon Way passes through the parish and runs along the eastern ridge of the hill, making use of old bridleways and the footpath through the churchyard to the village street. It is marked with yellow arrows and a stylised 'W' symbol.

Astley 🌿

From his garden at Astley Hall the late Stanley Baldwin wrote that he looked on 'a circle of beauty', and today the Astley he saw from the Abberley Hills to the river Severn still warrants that description, even though the orchards – plum, cherry, pear, and apple are all gone in the name of economic progress, and Lord Baldwin's Hall is now a nursing home. The urban sprawl of Stourport-on-Severn threatens the northern boundary and Shavers End quarry, a mere dent in the Premier's day, is now a gash a third of the way across the hill.

Astley is not a typical village. Large in area but having no centre, it is rather a collection of scattered hamlets, diverse in size and character which would seem to follow the pattern of the old manors, two of which are mentioned in Domesday Book. 'Eslei' was the Norman scribe's interpretation of Astley – the east 'leah' or clearing. The area is still well-wooded and retains signs of primary woodland.

'Eslei' was handed over to a Norman Priory, and today there is still a Prior's Well, some small remains of the monastic buildings, and a splendid, basically Norman church. On a south-facing hillside below the church is an overgrown area called the Vineyard, a relic of the French monks perhaps? Less than two miles to the east there is a very successful modern vineyard producing award-winning 'Astley' wine.

Astley still has its village church school, a late 19th century linear descendant of the original built and endowed by 'Ye pious and Charitable' Mrs Mercy Pope in 1743. The old school is now a private house and lies away across the fields reached only by footpaths but evidently was used because a second school room had to be build.

In the church are two painted tombs of the ubiquitous and recusant Blounts, and many manorial monuments. In the churchyard lies the tomb of Frances Ridley Havergal, a hymn writer at seven, who was born at the rectory, and before she died in 1879, asked to be brought back to a grave looking over the beautiful valley. This tomb is a place of pilgrimage for people from all over the world.

Near the War Memorial is the 1920s village hall – beginning to show its age but used still for the usual village activities.

17

Along the eastern boundary of the village beside a clutter of holiday chalets and caravans, and a few houses, flows the river Severn, once served by three village ferries and a ford/causeway at Redstone which carried an old road. Above the river here is a former hermitage – a network of caves, well in use in the 12th century and still occupied in living memory. Now would-be river crossers must go to a bridge at Stourport-on-Severn or Holt Fleet. Today the river, once so valuable for carrying goods, is again alive with boats – pleasure craft of all kinds.

Perhaps Astley's most notable son was 17th century Andrew Yarranton. He progressed from draper's apprentice to Roundhead soldier, and thence to tinplating, writing, iron-working, agricultural experiment and canalising rivers. He probably made the three locks on the Dick Brook so that iron ore could be carried by boat most of the way to a forge up the valley. The remains of his locks and forge are still extant. In the 18th century the Worcester Porcelain Company had a grinding mill by the brook and in commemoration the present company created an Astley design, named after the village.

Nancy Weaver, an early 19th century witch, lived at Bull Hill and was said to be able to stop teams of horses with one look. But she seems also to have been in great demand when the butter would not come or the bread refused to rise. A 'presence' is supposed to haunt the old Rectory and the vicinity of the church. At Weatherlane Farm, the householders seem to have a minor poltergeist which shuts doors, bangs on floors and has lately learned to alter alarm clocks.

The former stables of Glasshampton Manor House which was burned down in 1810, are now the home of a Franciscan brotherhood, a remote place of peace and retreat.

Today, it would be true to say that the 'born and bred' in Astley grow less and less. Astley is very close to the West Midlands conurbation and holiday-makers as well as commuters still find it a desirable place, to camp, caravan, visit or live in.

Badsey 🌿

Badsey is a village of contrasts. There are the old picturesque houses – the Manor House (the Seyne House), originally a convalescent home for the monks of Evesham Abbey, the beautiful Stone House of the Stuart period and several gracious Georgian houses. Then in the sheltered part of the village are the pretty black and white cottages which run down to the old silk mills and the brook. But the majority of housing is Victorian red-brick and smart modern estates. The old fruit orchards, which ran down to the brook, are now built on. They were playgrounds for generations of children until the 1960s and were a beautiful sight in the spring.

However, the quantity of housing means Badsey is a very lively village, full of children who attend the excellent local school, or nursery school, playgroup or mother and toddler group. Other Societies abound such as W.I., Young Wives, Mothers' Union, Over 60s, Red Cross, British Legion and two excellent charity raising clubs which are attached to the two local pubs.

Badsey's name originates from Badda (a chief's name) and 'eye' meaning island, as the brook circles the village. The old villagers say it is spoilt now the meadows and orchards have been swallowed up. They remember the days when the Flower Show was the high spot of the year, when almost everyone made their living from the land. Everyone knew everyone else and characters abounded. The aroma of new-made bread floated from the two bakeries and cider was made in the old cider press in High Street. True, they were lovely days but change is inevitable and there are still many characters in the village. The blacksmith's forge is worth a visit to hear all the gossip and to watch the ever busy Dick and David Caswell shoeing horses or mending or making tools or wrought-iron gates.

Badsey is lucky to have two good shops, a post office, a butcher, a garage, and a bank. However, the most central building of all is the lovely old church of St James, with its pretty churchyard and lychgate, recently the object of a restoration appeal. Its churchyard records generations past who loved and cared for the village. People use the pathway through regularly and sit on the many seats provided. The peal of bells are of high quality and are used by visiting ringers – much to the delight of some villagers, but to the annoyance of others.

Sporting facilities are exceptional for a village. Badsey Rangers football club has reigned for years, 'invincible in scarlet and black' on the recreation ground, but now Ballard's park is the largest complex. Originally land given by William Ballard for a cricket club, it now extends to hockey pitches for Evesham men's hockey, another football pitch for Badsey United and facilities for archery.

The market gardening has changed. As well as successful local growers, many large holdings are now run by Italian families growing peppers and aubergines as well as salad crops. The majority of residents are now commuters to jobs outside the village.

Barnt Green 🌿

Barnt Green's history as a village is little older than its oldest inhabitant. As long ago as 1846 it had a railway station and a station-master in a top hat, but for nearly half a century the station stood among fields, and in 1851 the population was 46.

There was a cottage pub called The Slipper because the beer-seller was also a shoemaker; there was, and still is, a handsome 17th century house, now an inn, and several old farmhouses. The Red House, is said to be haunted by the ghost of a love-sick maiden cruelly jilted by a young man living at the Elizabethan house across the fields.

By 1900 many large houses had been built on the slopes of the Lickey Hills, with smaller houses for their grooms and gardeners as well as for railway workers and work people at Bournville, the Austin Motor Company at Longbridge, and the factories at Redditch. Shops were opened in the village (one sold 'Fish, Game, Oysters in Season & Celebrated Cream Cheese') and a six-day licence was granted to the Victoria, originally built as a temperance hotel.

A weekly cattle market was held near the station, and animals were herded up the unpaved village street. Worthy ladies dispensed non-alcoholic refreshment to the drovers from a wooden hut.

By the 1920s Barnt Green had a church, a Friends' Meeting House, a Baptist chapel, a Working Men's Club, a Sports Club and a Church School, as well as many more inhabitants. There was a bowling green at the Vic, weekly dances at the Sports Club (1/6d a ticket and the men had to wear a dinner jacket) and the Cricket Club flourished.

Until the large sidings were removed in the early 1960s under the Beeching regime, the Royal train stayed overnight on several occasions, bringing King George VI and Queen Elizabeth and the present Queen and the Duke of Edinburgh.

The high railway embankment was a favoured place for the release of racing pigeons sent by train. Huge numbers would suddenly fill the air and as suddenly be gone.

Barnt Green is now largely a dormitory for workers in Birmingham, Bournville, Longbridge, Redditch and Bromsgrove, just as it has always been.

Belbroughton

Nestling in a valley on the lower slopes of the Clent hill range lies the village of Belbroughton. Through the centuries the village has been known by a variety of names, including Broctune, Belne, Bellem, Bryan's Bell and Bellenbrockton before finally becoming Belbroughton.

The earliest mention of the village was in AD817 but there could have been an earlier settlement. In 1086 there was already a priest and a Saxon church, which stood on the same site as the present Holy Trinity church. The church was later rebuilt by the Normans and some remnants of this structure still remain. The church has been altered over the years with large scale restorations in the 1890s. The tower clock was erected in celebration of Queen Victoria's Diamond Jubilee and the lychgate was built in 1912 and dedicated to Henry Charles Goodyear, a missionary from the parish. The giant chestnut tree on the south side, was recorded as being over 17 feet in circumference in 1850.

Across the road from the church is the half-timbered tithe barn, now used as a village hall. Further along is the village school, today accommodating children from 5 to 9 years old, with some 48 pupils. The oldest building in the village is the red, sandstone chapel built circa 1200 and which stands in the grounds of Bell Hall.

Despite all the new houses built in the village during the last 30 years there are fewer inns and shops serving the village today than in the 19th century. At one time there were at least 11 inns and alehouses but today only four remain. The Bell Inn, the oldest, and recorded as belonging to Sir John Conway in 1580, The Talbot Hotel and the Horseshoe Inn at the village square have survived along with The Queen's Hotel at the lower end of the village. The village today has only two grocery shops, a butcher, and a post office.

Belbroughton's sons and daughters have, over the years, emigrated to the far corners of the world. In 1787, one Sarah Bellamy, set sail for Australia, alas not of her own volition. Sarah, a 15 year old servant girl, was convicted of stealing a linen purse and money and sentenced to transportation to Australia, sailing with the First Fleet, and spending the rest of her life there. In 1987 when the Bicentennial celebrations were held at Portsmouth to mark the sailing of the First Fleet, two of Sarah's great-great-great-granddaughters from Sydney attended and then travelled to Belbroughton to see the birthplace of their ancestor. Belbroughton History Society welcomed them and erected a plaque on the village green to commemorate their visit.

Entering Belbroughton from Clent one sees a large painted sign depicting four village scenes and a man with a scythe. This sign was painted by a W.I. member and presented to the village by the W.I. in 1938. The man with the scythe was Isaac Nash, who made the firm of that name famous the world over for its crown scythes, hooks and hay-knives. He first took over a forge high up the Ram Alley Brook at Newtown in 1835 and employed just two men but by 1881 he owned all the forges and mills along the stream and employed 105 men and 5 boys. Nash Works finally closed in 1968 and the age old industry ceased.

Beoley

Lying at roughly 500 feet above sea level in the north-west corner of Worcestershire and on the very edge of Redditch New Town, Beoley is one of the earliest inhabited sites, and one of the most historic in the area. Its name probably comes from the Anglo-Saxon word for a honey bee 'beo' and 'ley' meaning a meadow or clearing. Hence a clearing in the forest where bees were kept.

Long before other churches were founded a chapel existed on Beoley Hill, probably to serve the Romano-British families who had settled in the area to take part in the local smelting industry or to serve the travellers along Ryknield Street which runs at the foot of the hill. This is now known as Icknield Street. An old saltway also ran through the village. An ancient earthwork sits atop the hill and somewhere in the same area a wooden motte and bailey castle was erected by the Earl of Warwick after the Norman Conquest, but was burnt down in 1309. The area to the south of Beoley was visited by early man on his hunting trips and a log boat, believed to be at least 4,000 years old, was found close to Beoley's boundaries in 1969.

Set in a picturesque churchyard with the vicarage close by, Beoley church is full of interesting and decorative features. It was founded in 1140 and has been added to many times since then. It is dedicated to St Leonard, the patron saint of prisoners and ironworkers. The church is chiefly notable for the tombs of the Sheldon family. The Sheldons owned Beoley Manor for many years and were responsible during the 16th and 17th centuries for introducing and promoting the art of tapestry weaving into England. Much of the work was done at nearby Bordesley Abbey and examples can be seen in the church and at the Victoria and Albert Museum.

The main house in Beoley is Beoley Hall which is now situated alongside the old Ryknield Street to the north of the church. The original manor house was probably closer to the church but, during the Civil War, the Royalist Sheldons were unable to resist the onslaught of Cromwell's troops and on the advice of Prince Rupert the hall was burnt down to prevent the enemy using it. Unfortunately the records and Court rolls were not removed beforehand and much documentary evidence was lost to posterity.

Streams that pass through Beoley feed the river Arrow. This river was the power for many mills in the area and Beoley Paper Mill and Beoley Needle Mill were two of them. The paper mill produced the special blue paper for wrapping the needles.

The main settlement of present day Beoley lies at the foot of the church hill to the east and is called Holt End. At the beginning of this century it boasted a post office, butcher, blacksmith, general store, Methodist chapel, village pub, school and a reading room. The latter was set up by the Carnegie Trust in 1904 and in the past few years it has been extended and refurbished to become Beoley village hall. It contains a large and much prized tapestry worked between 1937 and 1939 by W.I. ladies.

Although farming has been the main occupation in Beoley over the years, it has mostly a commuting population today. Redditch New Town is only one field away, but Beoley is a happy and thriving community and retains its character.

Berrow

Berrow, the next parish to Birtsmorton, has a fine medieval church with a Norman nave, chancel and doorway. A stone on the outside wall marks the grave of a father, mother and daughter, done to death one night over 100 years ago. Another tragic memory survives in the persistent tradition of the Nanfan Sermon which is preached every year. It is said that a lady whose lover was slain by her brother in a duel, was so horrified that she left £2 a year to the vicar for a sermon against duelling. Facts do not seem at first to bear out this story, for the Nanfan Sermon was first preached in 1745, nearly 100 years after the duel is supposed to have taken place, provided for by Sir John Nanfan. But historian Lees, writing in 1867 states, 'I have a copy of the will which proves the fact'.

Birlingham

Was Birlingham once the Gretna Green of the Midlands? The marriage register relating to St James' church shows an astonishing increase in the number of weddings celebrated in the church during the first 35 years or so of the 18th century. Hitherto the number per decade had been no more than 14. Then in the first four decades of the 18th century it rises to 17, 89, 102 and 74 entries respectively. In most of these cases both parties of the marriage came from places outside Birlingham – some from as far afield as Scotland.

Had this phenomenon anything to do with the curacy of the Rev Joseph Severn, who came to the village as rector in 1693? He died in 1745. After his death the number of weddings in the parish dropped immediately and the normal pattern was resumed. It remains a mystery why Rev Joseph Severn was able to attract so many, from so far afield, to marry in his church.

About 60 years ago an unusual event occurred in Birlingham which became headline news in local papers. It concerned a middle-aged, rather scruffy little man called Mr Pegram. He told the locals he was an artist and had taken up with an old couple called Day who lived in one of the last cottages in Nafford Lane.

At that time, a very good policeman stationed at Defford patrolled the village. PC Foster was the old fashioned type of policeman, big, burly and red of face. Despite his liking for cider and home-made wine he was a very intelligent man. He became suspicious of Mr Pegram and eventually he and the Inspector from Pershore decided to investigate. One morning six policemen hidden in a hedge at Rough Hill waited and when Mr Pegram appeared they pounced. In his canvas pack they found 57 forged half crowns and 10 florins. Another 200 were found when they searched his room together with a wonderful set of dies used in making the coins, a large stock of inferior metal alloy and a small furnace which fitted in the bedroom fireplace.

At his trial at Worcester Assizes in 1932, he was said to have travelled by bike to sell his coins for perhaps half of their face value to people out of work, and they turned up at Cheltenham, Birmingham, Tewkesbury and many other places around Evesham. Pegram was sent to Gloucester gaol and PC Foster was highly commended by his superiors.

Birtsmorton 🎑

Birtsmorton has a delightful timbered house, Birtsmorton Court, with a moat all round, which is partly 14th century. It was the home of the Nanfans and the gift of Henry VI to Sir John Nanfan, his squire. Cardinal Wolsey was chaplain to Sir Richard Nanfan, and tutor to his son. It is thought that the rise of Cardinal Wolsey may have been partly due to this Sir Richard, who introduced him to the king.

There is a secret hiding-place in the Court where Sir John Oldcastle was hidden when he was being hunted as leader of the Lollards, a religious movement repressed by Henry IV. He had escaped from the Tower and sheltered at Birtsmorton. Eventually he was caught and hanged in 1417 for heresy.

An interesting connection with history relates to the coming of the railway; William Huskisson was born at Birtsmorton and was the first man to be killed by a train.

The cross-shaped church is close by. Originally 14th century, a lot has been rebuilt. The table tomb is believed to be that of Sir Richard Nanfan. There is a magnificent tomb, with a carving of a ship, in memory of Sir William Caldwell, who commanded a squadron in the Baltic and died at Birtsmorton in 1718. He was the second husband of the last of the Nanfans – Catherine, a lady who married four times.

Bishampton 🎑

Bishampton has an attractive village street with some fine black and white properties, a modern shop and an inn, The Dolphin.

There are several small estates of modern houses and a fine spacious village hall which is 'The Villages Hall', thus providing also for Abberton and Throckmorton, each about two miles distant.

The name comes from the Saxon Bisacca and his settlement.

The church of St Peter is mostly 19th century but includes a font and doorway dating from the late 12th century.

Blakedown 🎑

Blakedown lies in the Green Belt, three miles from Kidderminster and is part of the parish of Churchill with Blakedown. The parish is recorded in the Domesday Book.

A turnpike road linking Kidderminster and Birmingham built in 1777 ran through Blakedown. There was a toll house at its junction with the Belbroughton Road, and with the coming of the railway, the owner of the Springbrook forge at the bottom of Forge Lane, made a short cut from there to the station to avoid paying toll on his goods. He planted this with trees and it is still known as The Avenue. Then, the coming of the Oxford, Worcester & Wolverhampton railway (known as the 'Old Worse and Worse' owing to its unreliable rolling-stock) through Blakedown brought many changes. Churchill became a quiet rural back-water while Blakedown developed rapidly.

The village lay on the saltway and from Roman times this brought links with the outside world. It was also famous for its water and lakes, made by damming streams from the Clent hills, which brought industry to the area even before the advent of the railway. The water powered the many cornmills and ironworks (making spades, shovels, and in the world wars, bomb casings).

In the 1930s water also brought workers from Lancashire and Cumberland for two months each year. They came to cut willow and make clogs. The water and the willow are still here, but no cutters now come. Instead, the lakes are used for fishing and, weather permitting, skating. Perhaps much more important, year after year, the swans and geese are a regular sight for a few months as they fly out across the village each day to their own chosen spot, and fly back to roost each night.

From being a truly rural village the years have brought many changes, particularly since the last war, when American troops were stationed here. A new council estate for Kidderminster was built in 1950. Private estates grew as land was made available, so that the village is now almost a dormitory area for the stock-broker belt of Birmingham! Despite that it is still a close-knit community, with many newcomers bringing young families, which helps keep the Church of England School (First) active.

One of the oldest houses is Harborough Hall, built in the 1600s, and for some time occupied by William Penn (who founded Pennsylvania, USA). On part of the land has been built a fine Sports Centre. There are two active churches; one, the mother church, serving Churchill, and one, Blakedown. Lord Cobham holds the living in both cases -- in earlier days, Blakedown was part of Hagley. Hagley Hall, Lord Cobham's estate, is on the boundary and Lord and Lady Cobham and their sons maintain their link and interest.

Being so near to Kidderminster, the village has to watch its Green Belt status and the progress and growth of the motorways which surround it.

The main Kidderminster–Birmingham trunk road runs straight through Blakedown, cutting the village in half and frequent repairs to the M5 mean that traffic is diverted through the village. Yet still it is surrounded by breathtakingly beautiful countryside. Steps have been taken to keep the many public rights of way fully open. There are ten pools in the vicinity, all of which are easily reached, several bridle paths, and the walking is easy.

Bockleton 🌿

The parish of Bockleton has been a farming community since Saxon times. This rural area in the west of Worcestershire, bounded to the west and south by Herefordshire, lies 700 feet above sea level. To the Normans the pastures and woodlands probably looked very much the same as they do today. Within 100 years of the Norman Conquest they built the nave of Bockleton church almost on the foundations of the previous Saxon church.

From then onwards, until the beginning of the 20th century, the church was largely maintained by the Lords of the Manor. They included names like Richard de Bockleton in 1174, the Barneby family in the 16th century, and after that, for many generations Bockleton was owned by the Childe and Baldwyn families.

Finally in 1864 Mrs Arabella Prescott came from London and bought the Bockleton and Hampton Charles estate. She lived at The Birches in Hampton Charles until her death in 1886. During those 22 years she built 22 houses, all of the same brick pattern. To make these bricks she brought two families from Staffordshire, the Abbotts and the Capewells, who made all the bricks in Hampton Charles. Old Bockleton Court was completed before her death, and became the home of the Prescott family. It is now a Field Study Centre run by the Birmingham Education Authority.

Bockleton Farm and The Hill Farm were at one time manor houses within the parish, the latter dating back to 1575. Cockspur Hall was, until the beginning of the Second World War, the Parsonage House, having been built by a member of the Baldwyn family about 1750.

In 1982, when the Lord of the Manor died, the manorial lands and farms were sold, mostly to sitting tenants. While remaining almost entirely a farming community, the nature of the hamlet is gradually

27

changing, and small businesses have been started. The small population now includes many young people, with young children.

The village hall, built about 1958, has become the focal point of the community. A play group is held there on two mornings a week, but since about 1960 there has been no school in the village. The old school building is now a private residence.

The only public transport is a weekly bus to Tenbury Wells. In 1984 the telephone boxes were removed. In 1987 the post office closed when Mrs Stallard retired after 50 years.

The community, however, is not a declining one, as the lack of these amenities might suggest. Rather does it prove that the population is sufficiently modern and prosperous to provide its own mobility and contacts with the world beyond its parish boundaries.

Bournheath

Bournheath is a village of about 800 inhabitants three miles north-west of Bromsgrove. The name is thought to come from the Barn on the Heath, the cruck barn to which this refers still being in existence and obviously a distinctive landmark many years ago. It dates from the 12th century and is said to be one of the oldest in Worcestershire.

Close at hand is Tuppenny Cake, a triangular island at a village crossroads and where the surrounding cottages had to pay a tuppenny tithe to their landlord, squire of nearby Fockbury. This ceased in the 1930s.

Farming and landwork were the traditional living in this quiet hamlet but as industry developed in the Midlands in the 17th and 18th centuries, so Bournheath eventually had its modest part to play and nail-making grew and flourished, providing a hard-earned income for many families. So poor were the rates of pay. however, that it meant very long hours and everyone from the oldest to the youngest helping with the work. The old nailers' cottages look very different today, attractively altered and enlarged, the town dweller's dream of a cottage in the country.

The population grew and for a number of years there were five shops in the village selling general goods, animal feeding stuffs, sweets and tobacco, paraffin and so on. Several made their own toffee and one enterprising shopkeeper made thick rice pudding and sold it in chunks. There was a bakery, a dairy, several coal merchants, a hay dealer, a blacksmith and even a shoemaker. The last remaining general shop closed in 1982. Likewise, two small glassworks on Parish Hill both producing coloured glass also disappeared years ago.

Fifty years ago nail-making had practically ceased but by then the Austin Works was well established and men walked to work there. Later on there was Garringtons, the engineers in Bromsgrove, and then Harris Brush Works at Stoke Prior.

There are three public houses in the village, The Nailers, the New Inn and the Gate, which used to be The Gate Hangs Well. The ditty

> The gate hangs well
> To no mans sorrow
> Pay today
> And trust tomorrow

could be seen on the sign outside until very recently. All three pubs were purely functional over many decades but now with alterations and extensions draw custom from far and wide with comfortable bars and lounges and restaurants to match.

Bournheath falls mostly into the parish of Catshill, but also into Fairfield. It has a Methodist chapel but no church of its own, no village policeman, no school and no 'Big House'.

The village hall, built in 1967 is alongside the playing fields in Claypit Lane, close by Bricklefields where around 100 years ago bricks were made for the local cottages.

The changing character of this pleasant village from mainly manual workers with their large families crammed into their small homes, to one considerably more affluent, is typical of many with its easy access to motorways and large towns. The professional, managerial and executive are a significant section here today, but there is still a good sprinkling of farmers, market gardeners, skilled craftsmen and others, including the retired.

The village hall is well used and host to numerous groups. Most years there is a Village Fete, Bonfire Night Party and a Christmas Dinner for the senior citizens amongst many other social activities arranged by the Village Hall Committee.

Bredon 🌿

'I wonder what that village is called?' – How many people have asked that question while travelling up or down the M5 motorway, and seeing, across the meadows and river Avon, the cluster of houses surrounding the spire of Bredon church.

The setting of the village is very beautiful. It lies on the southern edge of Bredon Hill, immortalized in A. E. Housman's poem *Summertime on Bredon*. The village is caressed by the river Avon, on its last stretch before joining the Severn at Tewkesbury, three miles away.

As a village it has a unique centre with its lovely church, ancient rectory, tithe barn, Old Mansion and Manor House. The church of St Giles, built about 1180, entered on the north side by a Norman porch, holds the interesting monument to the Reed family, benefactors of the 17th century almshouses, originally built for spinsters of the parish.

The large stone-built rectory adjoins the church, standing on the river bank. Two stone figures sit astride the roof, some distance apart, one Charles II, the other Oliver Cromwell. Rumour has it that should they come together, it will be the end of the world.

Bredon school was founded in 1718 by William Hancocks for 12 poor boys of the parish, to be taught, clothed and apprenticed. The last scholar apprenticed was in 1883. A second school was built by voluntary subscription in 1876, to educate girls aged 5 to 14, and boys. One thriving school remains.

Bredon derives from 'Bre', a Celtic word meaning hill, 'dun' Celtic and Anglo-Saxon means hill or down, so the name is a pleonasm, i.e. 'hill hill' or 'hill down'.

The village is well-known through the novels *Brensham Village* and the *Blue Field* written by local author John Moore. The inhabitants are fortunate to have a river on one side of the village, and lovely historic Bredon Hill on the other, sometimes called, 'The weather glass of the Vale of Evesham'.

> When Bredon Hill puts on his hat
> Men of the Vale beware of that;
> When Bredon Hill doth clear appear
> Ye men of the Vale have nought to fear.

Over the years, Bredon has seen changes in the employment of its residents. Like all villages in the Vale of Evesham, fruit growing, farming and smallholdings were the main sources of income for the men. The women also helped with the picking and packing of the fruit and vegetables. The young girls mostly found employment as domestic servants around the local area, some would venture to the bigger towns.

Sadly, for some, this way of life has changed. Much of the market garden land has been built on, doubling the village population. The 'Beeching Act' closed the railway station, to the regret of many villagers, leaving a derelict area. Fortunately for the village some enterprising men started fresh industries.

The village caters for most sporting needs: an excellent cricket club, bowls club, football and tennis clubs, sports field and a splendid village hall. The Community Care council does what its name implies, and really cares for people. The church plays a very important part in village life, having a large congregation well supported by young and older members.

Bredon's Norton is also in the parish, and has its own church, but shares one rector. The church is not dedicated to a saint, but is known as the chapel of ease to St Giles. This is a picturesque village and like the neighbouring hamlet of Westmancote, has cottages and houses of Cotswold stone and thatched black and white dwellings.

The 'King and Queen Stones' stand above Westmancote, two remarkable objects where a superstitious practice may have taken place. Kinsham and Bredon's Hardwicke complete the hamlets round Bredon.

Bredon village has its share of stone and thatched dwellings, one of its two attractive inns having a truly picture postcard image. Both these hostelries provide good food. There are also two excellent village stores, one having a post office and its own bakery.

Broadheath

The parish of Broadheath is of recent origin having been formed in 1952. Prior to this the area was part of the parish of North Hallow. The most populated part of Broadheath is the village of Lower Broadheath which lies on the B4204 from Worcester to Tenbury Wells. The southern part contains an area of common land and is geographically known as Upper Broadheath.

From Norman times the area consisted of small hamlets. Broadheath originated from squatters' settlements upon ancient manorial wastes of Hallow, but their status was regulated in 1816 with an official enclosure of common land. Other hamlets existed at Peachley, Eastbury and Lovington.

In 1840, it is recorded that in Broadheath there were three boot and shoe-makers, two wheelwrights and two blacksmiths and, in view of the small population at that time, it must be assumed they serviced an area well beyond the village. Today, all these have disappeared and the only industry is a large food processing firm at Temple Laugherne and a small Garden Centre. In 1904, there were two public houses, The Bell and The Sailor's Return, the latter is now a restaurant. There are now two more public houses – The Dew Drop in Bell Lane and The Plough in Crown East Lane. There are two general stores, one of which was originally Broadheath Bakery and now includes the post office.

The population has increased considerably in the last 30 years with much development around the whole of the parish, the majority of the occupants commuting to Worcester and beyond. The basic industry of agriculture and horticulture continues as it has for many years, the only change being the crops grown and milk production, beef cattle and sheep are the main usage of farm land.

A chapel of ease was erected about 1837 which is now part of the school buildings, and also a chapel belonging to the Countess of Hunt-ingdon's Foundation was built in 1825. It was not, however, until 1904 that a new church (Christ Church) was built. The village school was built in 1873 and enlarged in 1894 to accommodate 120 children and a further addition has been made in recent years.

The flavour of life in the parish today is greatly enhanced by the efforts of many people who promote and organise clubs, meetings and events for the benefit of all ages, from a Toddlers Group to the Over 60s Club, a Garden Club, Whist Drives and an annual Church Fete.

'Broadheath can claim a unique distinction as the birthplace of one of the greatest of English musicians, Sir Edward Elgar, M.O., Master of the King's Musick, Author of *Gerontius* and *The Apostles*, an honorary member of all leading Music Academies in both the old world and the new'. This account was written during Elgar's lifetime and today the birthplace is a museum administered by The Elgar Trust, much visited by music lovers from all over the world to see manuscripts and personal effects.

Broadway 🌿

If you read the guide books, almost without exception they approach Broadway from the south, coming in on the A44 down the tortuous Fish Hill, where, it is said, travellers used to make their Will before descending. But if you approach it from the opposite direction, your first view is of the northern ridge of the Cotswolds topped by the famous Broadway

Tower, built in 1798 by the Earl of Coventry to please his wife. On a clear day it is said that 13 counties can be seen from the top of the Tower.

On entering the village, one is immediately struck by the width of the main street, which is due to the fact that a stream lies below each side of the road making it, indeed, a 'broad way'. Broadway, or Bradweye to give it one of its earlier names, was granted a charter in AD 967 and over the centuries many notable people have stayed here.

Turn right at the village green and about a mile down the Snowshill road is the beautiful and ancient church of St Eadburgha. Next to it is the Gate House which is all that remains of the Court where Charles I stayed on two occasions.

Returning to the village main street, on the left-hand side is the Lygon Arms Hotel where both Charles I and Oliver Cromwell stayed – at different times one hastens to add! Then the White Hart, but later re-named the Lygon Arms, it is now one of Britain's most prestigious and oldest hotels being first mentioned in the Broadway parish register as a travellers' rest in 1532.

Broadway is reputed to have many ghosts. Legend has it that a lady was killed whilst hunting and her ghost still rides along White Ladies Lane, a deep gully which runs along the foot of Colliers Knapp at the top end of the village.

Most of the old shops have disappeared now, for instance the bake-houses where housewives used to take the Sunday joint to be cooked, the old saddler where the tackle was made on the premises, the blacksmith's with its open forge and the cider mills. Broadway does still retain some of its old traditions, such as 'Broadway Wake' the village fair which is still held on the village green each Whit Wednesday and Thursday. Gone though are some of the old characters of the village, such as the stout old lady rejoicing in the name of Mrs Fridlington who sold the most succulent faggots from her front room!

Broadway today is a thriving village, much visited by tourists, but lying as it does on the A44 is heavily burdened by traffic. It has changed greatly, as many villages have during the last two or three decades, but village life still goes on. Many of the old families remain, new ones have joined the village and many new friends have been made. Today it has churches of four denominations. It still has two village schools, two playgroups, a village flower show every September, Football and Cricket Clubs, a bowling green, Guides and Scouts, a Youth Club and a thriving WI. Broadway is still waiting for a bypass, as it has been for many years. When it does happen, who knows, the village may regain some of its former peace and tranquillity.

Broome

The civil parish of Broome is a small rural parish in the north-east of the county, an area a little under two square miles, and with a population of under 300. It comprises two old settlements, the village of Broome and the hamlet of Yieldingtree, but there are newer houses at Hackman's Gate and elsewhere along the main road. The ecclesiastical parish is much larger, with over twice the population, and extends right into the village of West Hagley to the north.

Although it has always been in the Diocese of Worcester, Broome was, until 1844, in the county of Stafford, and in earliest times was part of the Manor of Clent, when large areas were open common land on which the broom flourished. The Broome Enclosure Act of 1779 brought this into private ownership, and at that time the roads of today were laid out - Broome Lane, and the main Worcester Road, from the Spout (at the Cross Keys) to Hackman's Gate. The latter was built, so it is said, by French prisoners of war.

The village itself lies hidden from the major roads and is as pretty a village as one could wish, with snowdrops and daffodils along the verges in spring, a pond with mallard, Canada geese and water fowl, many fine trees, and well kept gardens with flowering shrubs. The school, which closed in 1933, was converted into a village hall. The little red-brick church, dedicated to St Peter, was built in 1780 and replaced a much earlier church of the 12th century, which had fallen into disrepair. In its beautifully cared for interior is the original font, and on the walls some interesting memorials, including an early 19th century memorial tablet carved by John Flaxman.

Before the last war the population of Broome was largely agricultural. Now many of the small farms have disappeared. Top Farm, Spring Farm and Lodge Farm are private dwellings. Manor Farm has become a Rest Home for elderly folk, as has Broome House. The Old Rectory, and more recently its replacement built in 1923, are both now private houses, for Broome is now a united benefice with the neighbouring parishes of Blakedown and Churchill. Most of the newer houses in the village, and the older ones which have been modernised or extended, are now occupied by commuters or retired people. Fortunately three farms are

34

still working – Broome Farm, Yieldingtree Farm, and Red Hall Farm, one of the oldest buildings in the village.

Burcot

Burcot is a small village which appeared in the Domesday Book under the name of Bericote – a combination of 'Byrig' meaning a fortified cottage or inhabited bower, and 'Cot'.

It lies about 2 miles north-east of Bromsgrove, and three miles from Barnt Green, very close to the famous Lickey Incline which is the steepest stretch of railway to be found on any main line in Great Britain.

In the centre of Burcot on the Alcester Road is the Burcot Forge, owned by Mr Ken White, a Master Blacksmith and Member of the British Artist Blacksmiths' Association. Originally Mr James Floyd from Ireland set up his anvil on this site in 1880 – his family had been 500 years in the farrier trade. The present forge was opened in 1902 by Charles Floyd.

The forge at Burcot

In recent years part of the substantial buildings has been let to other master craftsmen, including saddlers, furniture restorers, welders and toolmakers. People come from many parts of the Midlands and beyond to avail themselves of the diversity of skills offered. Ken White himself undertakes a tremendous range of work from massive ornamental gates with delicate wrought ironwork to miniature clamps for medical use. Parties are always welcome to look over the forge and many schoolchildren have been delighted to visit and to try their skills with the hammer. Ken White's wife, Nina is an accomplished silversmith and has a workbench in the forge.

The Alcester Road was a drovers' road, and women probably met near the forge over many years to meet the carrier's cart for salt from Droitwich and other essential goods.

> 'Long may the Forge stand,
> A symbol of the past,
> Adapting to the present,
> A link with the future,
> A focal point of village life.'

Burford

In the Domesday Book, Burford is referred to as Bureford – a village with a church and two priests. At the present time Burford is growing rapidly, and has a large industrial estate. The largest of the industries are involved with soft drinks, food processing, tungsten and precision tools, and between them employ large numbers of local people.

Agriculture is important. This is an area of mixed farming. Fruit and hops were once very important, but there has been a decline in fruit production. Many orchards have been uprooted and only old trees remain. Cider, made from certain types of apples, was the popular drink among farm workers, especially at harvest time. A mug of cider used to be offered as common courtesy when tradesmen or workmen called at the farm houses, or when it was that special time of the year, pig killing.

Sadly hop growing too is on the decrease and now only one hop-yard remains in Burford. This is the most northerly one in the country, although oast houses can still be seen at the farms.

In the 18th century a bounty was paid for the cultivation of hemp and flax and it is probable that Burford had flax-dressers, because the Linage

Farm is said to be so called from Linum – flax, which was once grown there.

Burford church houses many rich possessions. Much of its present appearance is due to Miss Georgina Rushout, who engaged an architect to enrich the building, in memory of her brother, the last Baron Northwick. The work was begun in 1889.

In the chancel is the Princess Elizabeth tomb. She was the daughter of John of Gaunt, Duke of Lancaster, and sister of King Henry IV. She married Sir John Cornwall, and he was champion tilter of England.

Also in the chancel is the heart tomb in memory of Sir Richard Cornwall, who died in Cologne in 1436. He willed his servant to bury his body there, but to enclose his heart in a lead casket and carry it to Burford to be buried.

Nearby, there is a life sized wooden figure on a wooden chest, Edmund Cornwall who died in 1508, at the age of 20. Another treasure is the triptych on the sanctuary wall. At the base of it, behind narrow doors, is a painting of Edmund Cornwall – lying full length in his shroud. He is said to have stood 7 feet 3 inches, and was known as the Giant of Burford.

Burford was the birthplace of Mrs Anna Williams, the oldest person with documented evidence of her birth. She lived for 114 years and 209 days. A sampler, worked by Anna in her childhood in one of the treasured possessions of Burford Primary School. The school is a new building in the middle of the housing estates which are springing up rapidly. The old school which Anna attended is now a toy factory.

Burford House, which stands near to the church, is famous throughout the country for its beautiful gardens, created by Mr John Treasure. Here one can see a range of unusual and interesting plants from all parts of the world. Over 100 varieties of clematis can be seen in the gardens, and the National Clematis Collection is now housed there.

Until the closure of the railway line from Kidderminster to Woofferton in 1962, Burford had a railway station – known as Tenbury Wells station. This followed in part the old canal, remembered now only by such names as Canal Cottages, Wharf Cottages and Weighing Machine Cottages.

A tollgate cottage still exists. A story is told that on one occasion a descendant of the famous Jack Mytton, took a friend in a dog cart full tilt over the Burford Tollgate. The horse got over clear, the trap too with the loss of the shafts. The blacksmith who lived close by came to the rescue, and a mug of cider closed the scene.

Changes in the village take place rapidly, and over the years the village carpenter, the blacksmith, the resident policeman and the resident district nurse have disappeared. There is a village store in the middle of the housing estate.

Bushley 🌿

The name of Bushley, Bisselega, in the Domesday Book, is probably derived from 'the meadow in the wood,' as it once formed part of Malvern chase.

The village is situated on the right bank of the Severn, approximately 2 miles from Tewkesbury. It is a community divided. The area clustering round the church is divorced by a long rise from Sarn Hill Grange Rest Home, the village green and houses nestling round the entrance to the park of Pull, an estate which originally formed part of the manor of Longdon.

There was a church here in the 12th century. The only relic remaining from the early church is the bowl of the font, which was discovered earlier this century in a farmyard. The next church is thought to have been built in the 14th century by Lord Edward Despencer and on its demolition in 1842 two of the windows were re-erected in the Moss Green shrubberies. Dr Edward Dowdeswell built the nave and tower of the new church in 1843 and the chancel was added in 1857 to designs by Sir Gilbert Scott, by William Dowdeswell in memory of his parents. In the interior of the church are interesting memorials to members of the Dowdeswell family, many of them having been laid to rest in the vaults beneath.

Bushley has one treasure connected with the church; a copy of Erasmus' paraphrases of the Gospels, printed early in the 16th century. The registers dating from 1538 are particularly detailed and interesting.

Close by the church, Wellingtonia House was formerly the vicarage and, before that, a farmhouse. The encumbent now resides at Longdon vicarage. Opposite the village hall is an Elizabethan house with extension, which formerly housed the village school, six pupils being paid for by Mr Dowdeswell and three by the curate. Reached by a lane at the side is Moss Green House, formerly The Pavilion, built in 1864 for the then local Squire and Member of Parliament, William Dowdeswell as a summer house. At the turn of the century it was used for dances and picnics, with boat parties moored on the river Severn.

38

Shepherd's Peace is a picturesque cottage on a corner. Down the lane opposite, at Bonners End, is Paynes Place, a fine half-timbered house looking over to Tewkesbury. It was built about 1450 by Thomas and Ursula Payne, supporters of the House of Warwick, Lords of the Manor at that time. It was to this house on an evening in May 1471 that two monks brought an exhausted fugitive from the victorious army of Edward IV after the Battle of Tewkesbury. Henry V's courageous Queen, Margaret of Anjou, spent the night at Paynes Place in a room known to this day as The Queen's Room, before continuing her journey in search of safety.

At the top end of the village is the village green. The tradition of village cricket is strong here and it is a lovely sight on a long summer evening to see the local team practising or engaging in friendly combat with visiting teams.

At Hill House Farm is the great barn where, until a few years ago, cider making survived in Bushley. Originally known as Severn Vale Cider, it achieved a wide reputation in the area and in 1930 it won the Champion Gold Medal at the International Brewer's exhibition.

Callow End 🦋

Callow End gets its name from the old Saxon word Calwe or Calwa, referring to a bare hillside, and even now the Old Hills at the edge of the village still have very few trees. There has been a settlement here since long before the Domesday Book was compiled.

Upon many modern maps Callow End is shown as Stanbrook, referring to the Benedictine monastery known as Stanbrook Abbey. The nuns have been in residence since July 1838, but the Tower which dominates the village was only built in 1871, by Pugin the Younger, the son of the Pugin who designed the Houses of Parliament. The clock strikes not only quarters, but every 7½ minutes, and the bells which call the nuns to church ring frequently during the day, which often surprises newcomers to the area.

There are several black and white cottages of great interest: one, The Glebe, is a cruck house, and an example of the oldest type of dwelling still surviving in England.

Today, the local hostelries are two in number, but in former years it took a greater number to quench the thirst of the locals! One of them, down at Pixham Ferry, was called The Boat and provided refreshment and entertainment for over 300 years.

The Pixham ferry boat was sunk during heavy floods in 1939 and unfortunately it was never replaced. It had for years been the only means of visiting the nearest doctor, resident in the opposite village of Kempsey!

Prior's Court is a very early manor house, famous for its ghost. She is known as the Grey Lady, and several sightings have been recorded. At one time it was difficult to keep servants in this house and one tenant actually asked for a reduction of rates for this reason! It is an interesting house, having a cockpit in the gardens for many years, and was for a time, the home of Sir Walter Monckton, friend of the Duke of Windsor.

Concerning the Old Hills, it was said that many of the cottages there were called 'squatter's rights', because if a man could build a chimney during the night and have his fire lit by morning, the surrounding land, as far as he could throw a hammer, was his!

In the past, hops have been a great source of income for the village. Until 1952, when mechanisation took over, workers from the Black Country livened up the village considerably as they took their annual holiday harvesting the hops. They slept in out-buildings at The Flax House in Beauchamp Lane. One supposes that the place has never been quite the same since their departure, though some hops are still grown and harvested here.

The Pound is still standing but these days no animals are retained there except those tied to the railings whilst their owners go to fetch the papers from the Pound Stores! The village is fortunate in that it has a bakery, a butcher, two garages and two general stores, one of which contains the post office. There is still a village school, a Working Men's Club, a good village hall, a really thriving Women's Institute, and last, but by no means least, a chapel of ease, dedicated to St James. Newcomers will find it a friendly and welcoming village, ready to offer help and friendship.

Callow Hill 🦜

Callow Hill is a small community and lies in the parish of Far Forest. It is situated about 3½ miles west of Bewdley on the A456 Tenbury Wells road on the southern edge of the Wyre forest. The area was originally part of the forest and has continued to develop because of its proximity to important cross country routes from earliest times. Before Bewdley bridge was built in 1447, the Heightington road was one of the main routes from Redstone ford on the river Severn, through Cleobury Mortimer and ultimately to Bangor, North Wales. The A456 passes over the newer (Telford) Bewdley bridge and is the main route from Birmingham to Wales.

The forest crafts have included charcoal burning, coppicing, timbers for ship-building and fuel, split-oak baskets, besoms, and bark-peeling for leather tanning. The underlying coal throughout the area has provided work and many people had to walk long distances to fetch coal from the pits to sell. The coming of the railway into the forest also brought work and an increase in population.

In 1856 the Royal Forester was reputed to be the oldest inn in the county. Its previous name was Mopson's Cross and it was held by the same family for 200 years. There was a tailor's shop opposite which later became a butcher's. There was a blacksmith's at the top of the lane to High Trees. People made their own bread.

Farming has played an important role in providing work for many people, sheep being prevalent. There are farming families in the general area who can trace their ancestry back through several centuries.

The Wesleyan chapel was founded in 1790 and at that time was further in the forest than the present Methodist church, built in 1864. There was also an Independent chapel at Lye Head founded in 1815. The area was originally in Rock parish before the church was built in Far Forest in 1844.

Catshill

Traditionally Catshill was an agricultural area, but in 1713 nailmakers came to the village. It was a home trade practised in small shops or sheds attached to the cottages. Working conditions were extremely poor, forges were rarely more that 15 feet by 12 feet, and the only means of ventilation was the door. Families all worked together, often more than 12 hours a day, receiving about 3 shillings per week. The following rhyme, in local dialect, by an anonymous author describes briefly the procedure of nailmaking:

> You get a bitter wier
> You put it in the fier
> You check it out
> You git a clout
> You got a nairl

The height of the trade's prosperity was the first quarter of the 19th century, but by 1830 the machine-made article was well established. From then on the hand-wrought trade began to decline. Agriculture still flourished in the 19th century and early 20th century in the form of market gardening.

Many religious denominations are represented in Catshill and the first Baptist chapel was opened in August 1828.The foundation stone of the parish church of Catshill, Christ Church, was laid by the Bishop of Worcester on 5th July 1837. This church is built of local sandstone in Early English style, and the nave window depicts St Chad, first Bishop of Mercia.

Some of the earliest buildings in Catshill are the nailmaker's cottages and farm dwellings of 17th and 18th century origin. Many of the cottages built in the 1830s were not at all like the picturesque black and white Worcestershire cottages, but constructed of red brick, usually comprising one room downstairs and one up. The space on the landing was often used as a sleeping area for children. Frequently families of ten or more occupied these small dwellings. Today these buildings are much sought after and when new owners extend and modernise they become attractive country cottages with individual character.

On the 7th November 1605, Catshill is recorded to have featured in the flight of the Gunpowder Plotters. They and other local Catholics fled to nearby Hewell Grange, and on to Holbeach House in Staffordshire, passing through Burcot, Catshill and Hagley.

The poet A. E. Housman had associations with Catshill. The Rev Thomas Housman, Alfred's grandfather, came to the parish church in 1838. As a youth A. E. Housman frequently read the lesson at Catshill church. About eight years ago, a flowering cherry tree was planted in Catshill churchyard by a party of Japanese, in his memory.

Many roads in Catshill have interesting and unusual names. Braces Lane may have been named after Walter Brace of Bromsgrove, who was fined in 1630 for refusing a Knighthood from Charles I. Cobnall Road, is possibly derived from Cob Nail, referring to round or cob headed nails. The Dock may have been the site of a sheep enclosure where lambs tail docking and sheep shearing took place. Dog Lane, now Meadow Road, was also called Watery Lane because the Salwarpe often overflowed its banks there.

The village hall, which was originally built in 1893, has recently been completely renovated and provides a very pleasant venue for many local organisations, including the WI. An annual carnival supported by many local organisations has been held since the Queen's Silver Jubilee celebrations in 1977 on the Geo-Wagstaffe Memorial Field.

Although so near to Birmingham, Redditch and Bromsgrove, Catshill remains an independent village, but with the close proximity of the M5 and M42 motorways, many residents now find it convenient to commute to these towns for their daily work, whilst still enjoying the friendly village life-style of Catshill.

Chaddesley Corbett 🌿

The gentle curve of Chaddesley Corbett village street with its harmonious mix of architectural styles from Tudor, through Georgian and Gothic to the present day, is, as it has been for centuries, the centre of a large parish which includes eight smaller settlements, just as in the Domesday Book eight 'berewicks' were mentioned.

In Saxon times the village was just Chaddesley. It was not until the manor passed into the hands of a Norman family, the Corbetts, that Corbett became part of the village name. It was this family that gave the village its present shape, laying out the plots for houses and gardens exactly as they are today.

The Corbetts were rich and ambitious. As a family, they were largely responsible for the rebuilding of the famous church, the only church in England to be dedicated to St Cassian and described by John Betjamin as 'the best example of 14th century work in the county with a 12th century font of pre-Conquest design'.

Although, as in any contemporary village, a large number of its inhabitants are 'in-comers' and usually commuters, the village works together in a most exemplary way. The village hall was given to the village to celebrate Queen Victoria's Jubilee and is in constant use with an active Sports Club and special events such as fireworks parties and several point-to-points each year. There is also a weekend Festival of Early English Music with concerts held in St Cassians and in the Roman Catholic Church of St Mary's, Harvington, attended by people from all over the country.

Although agriculture and horticulture are strong in the parish, with the advent of modern farming methods, fewer employees are needed, and the majority of residents work outside the parish, many in the carpet industry in Kidderminster, or in a professional capacity in the Black Country or Birmingham. For many centuries, scythe-making flourished

Chaddesley Corbett village street   Susan Sha

in the hamlet of Drayton, now on the identical site there is a thriving agricultural engineering business.

Within recent living memory, the street provided a shoe-maker, a tailor, a saddler, a maltster and several other trades. These have gone and their houses and shops are now very desirable residences, but there is still a long established general stores and post office. There is also a first rate butcher-cum-greengrocer, again on a site where there has been a butcher for at least 400 years, several builders and decorators, a petrol station and two garages for repairs, but public transport is poor.

Chaddesley people have always been noted for their independence of thought and this is exemplified by the story of Harvington Hall, the moated manor house in the hamlet of Harvington which was a centre for Catholicism all through the years of persecution. The Hall has several ingenious hiding places and was a refuge for many Catholic priests, including Saint John Wall, the last Catholic martyr in England.

44

Charlton

Charlton (near Cropthorne) is a very pretty village with Merry brook running parallel to the village street past the Gardener's Arms. Grassy banks, a seat, and some well kept cottages across the brook enhance the local scene.

There is a shop and a post office. Market gardening is still continued, and some agricultural activity is very noticeable.

Charlton Manor, now a small development of modern houses, was the home of the Dyneley family. Tombs bearing the family coat of arms are to be seen in nearby Cropthorne church and also on the front of a house in Hanley Castle.

Childswickham

Nestling in the Vale of Evesham and just two miles from Broadway lies the old picturesque village of Childswickham. The name Childswickham is believed to have derived from 'Child', the young son of a nobleman, 'wick', a clearing in the wood and 'ham', short for hamlet. Its history can be traced back to Roman times as coins and pottery of this era were found in fields on the old Roman road from Worcester to London which came through the village.

The village has a population of approximately 700 people and is surrounded by market garden and farm lands. The old houses are built in red brick, black and white half timber, thatch and Cotswold stone giving an interesting contrast in colour and design.

The 15th century spire of the original Norman church, St Mary the Virgin, is a local landmark and can be seen for several miles. The church contains a very unusual font and has a peal of six bells which ring out far and wide across the countryside.

The old village centre was situated around the Cross, 300 yards from the church. It was erected by the De Beauchamp family in the 15th century. The original was destroyed by the Puritans and later replaced with an urn from the churchyard. The Mill House lies between the church and the Cross and was in use until 1930. The last miller was Fred Newbury and is well remembered by older residents. The Old Manor House, built of Cotswold stone, stands adjacent to the Cross and dates back to the 14th century. It is the oldest house in the area.

A stream meanders through outlying fields and gardens of several cottages until it reaches Childswickham House, once called the 'William Mary House'. It was here in the 1870s that things went 'bump in the night'. The Blue Lady was often seen at one of the bedroom windows. One family decided to hold an exorcism and 12 parsons from parishes in the vicinity were invited to perform this ceremony. The old folk of the village said that if one of the parsons died within a year of the exorcism, the ghost would not disappear. One did!

During the last 20 to 30 years market garden land and orchards have become building sites. All 'in-filling' properties are built in reconstituted Cotswold stone and blend in very well with the character of the old residences. Of course this means that people from various parts of the country have settled here but the local dialect still remains and is called 'Aserm Grammar'. An example of this is as follows:- 'Wur bist thee a gooing' and 'Ow bist getting ou you'. Upon hearing this a number of times, one can eventually give an intelligent reply!

Many people in the village still work on the land and lorries laden with vegetables can be seen taking their produce to local markets. The majority of workers travel to Evesham, Stratford-Upon-Avon, Worcester and Cheltenham to a variety of occupations in offices, factories, shops etc.

There were more amenities in Childswickham 50 years ago than there are today. The village had a school, bakery, provision store, post office, blacksmith and miller but, alas, all have disappeared. The villagers now travel to Broadway or Evesham for their shopping needs.

Churchill

A very small hamlet of about a dozen houses and the imposingly named church of St Michael's Churchill in Oswaldslow. The 'church on the hill', and it shows – for miles and miles! There are two working farms and much pastoral land in the area.

Claines

Claines lies to the north of Worcester, part of it being within the city boundaries and part administered by the Parish Council of North Claines and Wychavon District Council.

The ecclesiastical parish is centred round the church of St John the Baptist, most of which was built in the 15th century on the site of a smaller one built in the 11th century by St Wulstan, last of the great Saxon bishops of Worcester. Earlier still was a Saxon church and the first known priest in Claines was Behstan, named in a document dated AD 957. The church also has some 19th century additions.

Claines was originally a chapelry to St Helens in the centre of Worcester, but in 1218 became a separate parish divided into several hamlets and including the ancient manor of Northwick. It included the present parishes of St George's with St Mary Magdalene, St Stephen's and St Barnabas', Rainbow Hill. Thomas Morris, vicar of Claines in 1689, was one of those who refused to take the Oath of Supremacy to William III and was deprived of his living. He is said to be the person buried in Worcester Cathedral under a gravestone inscribed, at his request, only with the word 'Miserrimus'.

Sir Edward Elgar's maternal grandparents are buried in Claines churchyard. Within the churchyard the Mug House has stood for centuries. In recent years during the work on this house an ancient crozier was discovered. This is now in the care of the Bishop of Worcester and is used at Christmas time by the Boy Bishop of Claines.

Within the parish lies Porter's Mill with its old half timbered house. Here, Queen Elizabeth I is said to have spent a night in 1574 during one of her royal progresses. This was still a working mill within living memory as was nearby Mildenham Mill.

The parish includes the ancient manors of Northwick, once the home of the Bishops of Worcester, and Bevere, a possession of the Benedictines of Worcester until 1542. Nearby Bevere Island has twice been used as a refuge for the people of Worcester, once from the Danes in 1041 and once in 1637 from the plague which swept through the city carrying away a fifth of the population.

Claines is bounded on the north by the parish of Hindlip well known for the fact that the first Hindlip House built by John Habington, a staunch Roman Catholic, was associated with the Babington Plot, an attempt to assassinate Queen Elizabeth I and put Mary Stuart on the throne. The house was later associated with the Gunpowder Plot of 1605. The new Hindlip Hall, built in the 1820s on the site of this ancient building, is now the headquarters of the West Mercia Constabulary.

Cleeve Prior 🦎

Cleeve Prior, 200 feet above the Avon, at the extreme eastern side of Worcestershire, is one of its smaller villages (population about 500 in 1987 and 108 in Domesday) but full of interest with a long history.

With its comparatively mild climate, the chief 'industries' used to be farming and market gardening – acres of fruit and vegetables were produced by the growers. But recently livestock farming has declined, cereals often replace cattle and sheep in the fields and there are fewer orchards, hedgerows and birds.

When in 1775 the strip cultivation and common lands were enclosed the whole appearance of the village was changed, but an equally great transformation came 200 years later when, tragically, Dutch Elm Disease killed thousands of trees – including the 300 year old giant on the Green.

Throughout the years Roman 'finds' have been frequent; 'the Greatest Hoarde' of gold and silver coins (circa 400 AD) ever made in Britain (until 1987) being by Quarryman Sheppey in Froglands Fields in 1811.

A second, rather gruesome 'find' in 1824 was down by the Old Mill (demolished after World War Two). Numerous skeletons were unearthed – probably Simon De Montfort's soldiers fleeing from Evesham, drowned crossing the river – which were re-buried under the Pilgrim's Praying Cross base, above the Nature Reserve Notice.

After Dunkirk, another 'unique' episode occured. The village woke one morning to find the Green covered with exhausted soldiers, who remained as Cleeve Prior's guests for a week . . .

As long ago as AD 872 Ethelred (Alfred's brother) 'gave the Manor of Cleeve to the Prior of Worcester' – hence its name, and 700 years later, Henry VIII 'presented' it to their Dean and Chapter! Finally, the Ecclesiastical Commissioners took it over in 1855. However, in 1915 the Hiorns, last of the Holtom family, who were tenants of the Manor for 100 years, bought the freehold.

St Andrew's church and the manor house, both on pre-870 sites, are the only large buildings in Cleeve Prior and were once the focal points of village life. The 15th century tower was also the Watch Tower in early days, and its base was used for sharpening arrows!

The church, manor and all other original houses are built of the attractive gold/grey stone from the Quarry Lane area, as are the inn, forge, cider mill, bakery, cobbler's and weaver's barn – all now private houses. Newer brick houses have gone up in 'gaps', or have been built in small groups further away.

In the church the magnificent tapestry altar frontal, worked by the Women's Fellowship, was designed by the vicar, (shared with Littleton) Richard Evans. He is not obliged to 'present a peahen every Christmas to the Church in Worcester' as were his early predecessors! There names hang in a list, unbroken from 1308, near the old font, alongside a 'Pictorial Survey' of the village – 870 to 1970.

A village Flower Festival in 1979 provided the carpet, beneath which are the Bushell graves. They lived in the Manor from 1545 for over 200 years and contributed Cleeve Prior's most noteworthy citizen – Thomas Bushell, buried in Westminster Abbey 'for Services to the Nation'.

Clent 🦢

Clent is one of the very few places in the country which is spelled the same today as it was in the Domesday Book. The twin hills of Walton and Clent are situated right on the south-west edge of the Black Country and form a wonderful recreation area for walkers and riders.

The village was once part of the Forest of Feckenham. A royal palace and shooting lodge were reputed to have been built on the slopes and Clent was designated a Royal Borough. This meant that the inhabitants were able to visit other areas without paying tolls. The living was, and still is, in the ecclesiastical patronage of the Lord Chancellor.

Within the parish boundaries are seven hamlets about half a mile apart from each other. There is St Leonard's Square, where a church has stood since 1199 and where there were two schools, one founded by John Amphlett in 1705 and the other by the Durant family in 1863. Both were replaced in 1974 by a new First School in Holy Cross. Walton Pool (which has no pool!) and Rumbow lie to the east, Adam's Hill and Lower Clent to the west, High Harcourt to the north and Holy Cross to the south.

Holy Cross is the centre of activities, the post office, paper shop, hairdresser, butcher and fireplace shop are there, also the Roman Catholic church, which was once a malthouse. The Bell and Cross public house stands on the corner, on the site of the last resting place for the pilgrims, before they made their way through the hills to worship at the shrine of St Kenelm, at the top of the pass.

The parish boundary between Clent and Romsley runs through the graveyard of a small church erected to the memory of Kenelm, the boy King of Mercia. He was murdered by his sister Quenrida and a spring

Holy Cross Green, Clent

gushed forth on the spot where the foul deed was thought to have been committed.

Nail-making was a cottage industry years ago and scythe mills were dotted along the course of the stream. The Vine Inn at Clatterbach was once a watermill and its cellars are still cooled by waters from the mill race. Today, most of the working population have to commute to nearby towns for employment.

The Sunfield Home for severely mentally handicapped children is a settlement run by the supporters of the philosophies of Rudolph Steiner. It is situated at the foot of Adam's Hill in spacious grounds which include what looks like a ruined castle, but is really a folly. Several of the larger houses in the district have been converted into nursing and rest homes for the aged.

There are many flourishing organisations in the village, including the Gardening Club and Women's Institute who jointly run the Annual Flower Show. The two fairs which were granted by charter long ago, no longer take place, neither does the custom of hauling branches of oak trees up the church tower on Oak Apple Day.

In the early 1900s a feud arose between the Squire and villagers, who considered he was enclosing more common land than was his due. The matter was taken to court and much to his annoyance Mr Amphlett lost the case. The family had been generous benefactors in the past and stung by what he thought was ingratitude by the villagers, Mr Amphlett vowed to do no more philanthropic deeds. Shortly afterwards the staff of Clent House and sundry outdoor employees such as gardeners and game keepers were ordered to attend all the church services and sit in the choir stalls. This they were perfectly entitled to do as the family were possessors of the Rectorial Tythe at the time of the Dissolution of the Monasteries, which made them owners of the chancel. After a while, the Squire now being domiciled elsewhere, the staff attendance began to fall away and soon the choir was able to resume its customary seats. One Sunday morning however, early worshippers were dismayed to find that during the night the chancel seats had been chopped to pieces, only the ends of the pews remained standing. School benches were put in the empty spaces which the long suffering choir sat on during services until the last of the Amphletts died. The heirs to the estate, wishing to pour oil on troubled waters, offered the deeds of the chancel to the church on the understanding that the Amphlett tombs and memorials remained undisturbed. This was happily agreed upon and in 1956 the sanctuary and chancel were renovated, the choir provided with new stalls, and peace was restored.

Most of Clent is in the care of the National Trust or in the Green Belt and Conservation Area, and its inhabitants fondly hope that nothing will happen in the foreseeable future to change the picturesque rural atmosphere of this delightful spot in which to live.

Clifton-upon-Teme 🦜

The village stands high above the river Teme amidst unspoilt countryside, with extensive views of the Malverns, the Clee Hills and Herefordshire.

The Saxon settlement known as Cliftun-ultra-Temedam was first recorded in AD 934 but there is evidence of earlier occupation. In the late 13th century Henry III granted borough status to the small town. This honour carried the right to hold a weekly market and a yearly four-day fair. Travellers came from great distances selling every kind of merchandise. The merchants met in the Guildhall which was also the manor house and court, later being used as a hostelry and known today as the Lion Inn. Court matters were often decided under an oak which stood on the green opposite the inn. The present chestnut tree replaces one which was blown down in 1877 and is still a focal point for the village.

A new and powerful family moved to the village. Ralph de Wysham and his wife settled at Woodmanton Manor and raised their family. The younger son, John, rose to the important position of Steward of the Household to Edward III. He rebuilt Woodmanton and also added the south aisle to the church, placing there a stone effigy of a crusader knight, possibly his father. There is a legend that Ralph de Wysham died under a yew tree on the estate and that his faithful dog refused to leave his master. Even today some villagers feel a strange power when passing the old tree.

Other stories abound of strange sightings of ghosts in or near the village. Some say that the sound of phantom horses has been heard and also that a white lady has been seen bending over a baby's cot. A nurse from the Civil War is reputed to have been seen, and also soldiers in the steep woods leading down to Ham Castle, another manor house which was bombarded and besieged by the Parliamentary army.

With the coming of the Industrial Revolution changes occurred and many families left the land to seek employment in the Black Country. Clifton remained a typical rural village with the Annual Wake still being held – a reminder of its medieval status as a borough. The cattle market and sheep fair took place until the early years of this century. The school was opened in 1844 and still provides education for children from the surrounding villages.

Many men left Clifton to serve in the two World Wars and the women also played their part in forming a Women's Home Guard and also in making parts for land mines. The arrival of electricity, mains water and sewerage brought Clifton, eventually, into the 20th century.

The area became a favourite venue for walkers and a branch of the Youth Hostels Association was opened, giving a welcome break to young people from the towns. People still travel from all parts of the country to see the blossom in the orchards which encircle the village.

Clifton is now designated a Conservation area and the grouping of the church, the inn, the school and the village green makes a delightful picture. The main street contains a charming mixture of architectural styles reflecting the long history of the village. There has been some new development in two small estates and that has helped to support the local shops – a butcher, post office, general store and garage.

The population is now about 600 and fewer people are engaged in farming. The lively, friendly community supports many organisations, including the WI, the Royal British Legion, an over 60's club and a drama group.

52

There is a great pride in the village and the whole community is pleased when an award is gained in the Best Kept Village or Churchyard competition. The many hanging floral baskets in the village street are a wonderful splash of colour each year as is the opening meet of the Clifton-on-Teme hunt on the village green.

Although Clifton has lost the importance it once enjoyed, it remains a very attractive village. Pride in its history was very evident when a pageant was staged a few years ago. It was said then that 'Clifton-upon-Teme is a village with a heart – a heart that has been beating for over a thousand years'.

Cofton Hackett 🌿

Cofton was first mentioned as early as AD 780 when King Offa granted land to the monastery church and the Anglo-Saxon Chronicles confirm this in 849.

Historically it has associations with several distinguished families, including the Leicesters and the earls of Plymouth. King Charles I stayed with Thomas Jolliffe at the Hall on the night of 14th May 1645 and before the Royalists marched towards Chester on 15th May, they set fire to the Hall to prevent it falling into the hands of the Parliamentarians. It was rebuilt in the early 19th century, but still contains a very fine 14th century hammer-beamed hall and outside the present building traces of older foundations remain.

The district remained mainly agricultural, but in the early part of the 19th century nail makers began their trade, and several of their cottages still remain. These tradesmen would have had to walk many miles to the Black Country to obtain the materials for their work which was hard, dirty and poorly paid. Nail-making finished by about 1912. In 1820 the Birmingham to Worcester canal was opened and a little later Cofton and Bittell reservoirs were built. These now provide a wonderful source of bird life, fishing and sailing activities.

Cofton is now a mainly residential area situated on the borders of Hereford/Worcester and the City of Birmingham. On the side nearest the church there are still a few farms and crossing the road you reach the broad-leaved woods of the Lickey Hills. These hills were mainly given, though some were purchased, to provide a permanent open space for the citizens of Birmingham. From time to time various 'improvements' have been suggested, but so far local people have managed to keep the open spaces open for all to enjoy.

A well known local character was 'Blackberry Jane'. If Blackberry Jane had lived in a town, she would have been designated as just another 'bag lady' but here everyone knew her tall, spare, upright figure, dressed in many layers of skirts and coats; always carrying two bulging bags and with many other oddments tucked into her bosom. Somewhere locally she had a family but one old lady remembers being at school with her, where she was a very irregular pupil, so wandering must have come early to her. She got her name of 'Blackberry Jane' or 'Blackberry Annie' as some called her, from the fruit she used to pick and sell from door to door in the autumn.

In 1971 Cofton Hackett got its village hall, this had long been campaigned for by local residents and many organisations worked long and hard to get it built, stocked and paid for. It houses many local groups and organisations and has recently been extended.

Conderton 🦢

Conderton is a small hamlet on the southern slopes of Bredon Hill with a population of 72. On the Hill there is Conderton Camp, first built in the 2nd century BC as a cattle enclosure. In the next century a drystone wall was constructed on the northern side of this area and a village was built in this enclosure.

Most of the hamlet is owned by the Holland-Martin family. Farming still continues in Conderton, one family having rented and farmed here for over 100 years. At one time nearly everyone was involved with agriculture, but nowadays very few people have connections with farming.

Conderton used to have its own post office, shoe mender, small shop and bicycle repairer, but these have all gone. There was also a wheelwright and a blacksmith, but the forge is now a thriving pottery. The Yew Tree Inn until recently had been owned by the same family for over 70 years, having previously been a farm. The Yew Tree Garage, owned by a member of the same family, still continues to operate. The coal merchant's business has ceased, and in its place is a small factory producing clothing.

Cookley 🦢

Cookley, part of the ancient parish of Wolverley (mentioned in Domesday Book) became a parish in its own right when the parish church of St Peter was built in 1849, largely through the generosity of the late William Hancock Esq and the efforts of the villagers of that time in subscriptions and fund raising.

The Methodist church celebrated its 175th year in Cookley in 1987. A new Methodist church was dedicated in Lionfields Road in September 1973, and the old church, after a life of 154 years in Castle Road, was demolished.

While not a 'picture-postcard' village, Cookley is surrounded by beautiful countryside. The church, school, and parish hall in Lea Lane, which leads on to the playing fields, are in close proximity to the village square. The square contains Swift's the butcher, Wren's the cobbler, Bell's the grocer, Hall's the newsagent, Scott's the fish shop and the post office stores. The latter was the village bakery in the 1920s. Also in the village square are the Bull's Head and the Eagle & Spur public houses, with the Red Lion a little way along Castle Road. Coupled with the Rock (now the Portalet) and the Anchor Inn in the closely adjoining hamlet of Caunsall, these hostelries were very much a part of village life in the past, as they still are today.

The playing fields overlook beautiful countryside, with views of Wolverley church, Trimpley, Blakeshall and Kinver Edge. The river Stour follows a winding course through the parish, and part of Brindley's Staffordshire & Worcestershire Canal lies between the playing fields and the river. The canal passes under Bridge Road through a 65 yard tunnel, the oldest in Worcestershire. The Elan aqueduct has for many years carried water from the Elan Reservoirs to Birmingham over the canal at Cookley. At present these water pipes are being transferred underground beneath the canal.

In 1950, through the fund raising efforts of the villagers and subscriptions, the excellent playing fields were purchased for the use of the village in perpetuity. In 1977 the Sports & Social Club was officially opened. The Parish Hall was opened in 1933, and here again the money for the building was raised in the village. The Parish Hall and the Sports & Social Club are the home base of many village organisations.

There has been a works in Cookley since 1650 when John Knight opened his ironworks and forge in the hollow at the lower end of the village adjacent to the river Stour. The river at one time was diverted through the works to provide power for the machinery. In 1860 a process for tinplating iron sheets was invented and the name of Cookley 'K' Tinpot became world famous. The site is now occupied by Steel Stampings Limited.

In the 1880s the works closed down, creating a recession and hard times for the Cookley people. Some families left the village, others let their spare rooms as holiday accommodation and visitors from the Black Country and Birmingham came for their holidays. Campers came to the Lock Meadow as late as the 1960s.

In the 1930s and later in the 1950s more houses were built and the village expanded. Today many local residents commute daily to Birmingham and the surrounding districts by car and train.

In spite of its close proximity to Kidderminster, Cookley still remains very much a village community. Its life is still centred round the church, chapel, parish hall, school and playing fields. The fund raising still goes on but everyone works together and enjoys it which makes Cookley a pleasant and happy village in which to live.

Cropthorne 🦜

Cropthorne is one of the most attractive of the Worcestershire villages and its black and white cottages and houses are often featured on postcards and calendars.

The village, comprising some 220 households, lies mid-way between Pershore and Evesham, and is set in the heart of agricultural land, market gardens and orchards. There are now fewer fruit trees and more buildings than there were two decades ago, and fewer people working on the land. Nevertheless the village proudly retains its character and remains a friendly close-knit community with life revolving round the church (where the bells still ring) the village school, the village hall and playing field, and the post office and stores.

The church dates from Norman times, and it contains some interesting features and tombs. An object of great interest is the head of a large Saxon Cross, which was found embedded in the south wall in the 18th century. This was removed and is now set on a plinth in the north aisle, thus enabling the intricate carving of birds, beasts and foliage to be admired from all angles. Names of families who have contributed much to the life of the village over the years are recorded on the various

memorials – the Hollands, Dingeleys, Tarplees, Forresters, Meakins and Croppers and many others. Some of their descendants are still in the village today, keeping up the traditions and making their contributions to village life.

The name Cropthorne is thought to have originated from a thorn hedge which marked the boundary between Croppa's land and the next village. Cropthorne is mentioned in the Domesday Book, but its history can be traced back further, to the time when Offa, King of Mercia, presented the village to the Priory of Worcester in AD 786.

There are many interesting buildings, one of them is Holland House. Formerly three cottages, this property was given to the Diocese of Worcester after the Second World War, by Mrs Ellis Holland. It is now leased by the Diocese to an independent trust and is run as a Retreat and Conference Centre. Many thousands of people now visit and stay at the Centre each year, participating in a variety of activities, benefiting from the atmosphere and enjoying the delightful Lutyens garden which surrounds the building. Perhaps Mrs Holland never wanted to leave – or is she just curious? Her ghost is reported to have been seen in the library not long ago.

The village has some tales to tell about a 'grey lady' who has appeared from time to time, but one of the strangest apparitions must be that of a soldier, whose uniform was identified as being from a Welsh Regiment at the time of the Battle of Worcester.

There are many village pastimes – there is a flourishing WI – combined with the neighbouring village of Charlton. Indoor bowls is a popular activity, there is a Bridge Club, a village choir and an enthusiastic scottish dancing group.

An event which draws the whole village together is the annual 'Walkabout' which takes place on the first Sunday and Monday in May. On these two days the village plays host to some 3000-4000 people who come to wander round and admire the beautiful gardens, some of which slope down to the river Avon and have magnificent views across to the Malvern Hills. The 'Walkabout' is a corporate effort by the community to preserve their heritage, but it also allows many people to join with them to become part of this beautiful village for a day.

Crowle 🐛

The earliest reference in Anglo-Saxon literature refers to Crohlea which may mean 'a place of clay', but another explanation of the Saxon word Croh is crocus. In the Saxon Charter of AD 846 there are references to 'where the saffron or crocus grows'.

Agriculture has provided a number of jobs for the men and boys in the past, on the various farms around the village. Some men also worked on the roads and later some found employment with the railways. Wages were low and to help supplement the men's wages, the women of Crowle made a little extra working for the flourishing Worcester glove trade as out-workers. This started in the 1800s when most of the gloves were hand sewn, but gradually machines were supplied to the women.

Today most of the farms have been absorbed into just three or four large ones and mechanisation means very few jobs. The gloving went after the Second World War and even the hops are picked by machines now. This means that Crowle has become mostly a commuter village, and even the children are bussed out to school after the age of 9.

Like most villages Crowle used to be self-sufficient and sustained 4 grocers, 3 bakers, 2 butchers and a shoemaker and repairer. Two blacksmiths, a tannery, and an undertaker, who made his own coffins and was also the verger. In the 1850s there was even a lady blacksmith, Sarah Dunslow. There was a policeman, a doctor and a bone-setter. Two carriers operated here and took passengers into Worcester before the coming of the bus service after 1918.

Crowle still has its village stores, a garage, post office, pub, school, hairdresser and a riding school which provides riding for mentally and physically handicapped children. It also has a dentist and a poultry farmer, and an active amateur dramatic society.

Entertainment was provided by various outings and fetes. The Forrester's Friendly Society had a brass band, which led processions through the village on fete days. The children danced around the Maypole on May Day and Empire Day was another school holiday.

One of the biggest social occasions was the Spring Steeplechase Meeting which took place around Climbers Hill. Coach loads of spectators arrived from near and far to enjoy the day. The main race was for the Lady Dudley's Challenge Cup. This was transferred to Chaddesley Corbett after the war.

The parish church of St John the Baptist was rebuilt in 1881 and

A Chartist Cottage, Dodford

founded sometime after 1184 for a community of Augustinian canons. By 1464 there was only one canon left and it was taken over by Halesowen Abbey. After the Dissolution in 1538 it became a farm and is now a delightful warm red brick and timber house.

Another building of interest is the parish church. This building, constructed on a new site at the eastern end of the village in 1908, replaced an earlier one which was built where the village hall now stands. It is said by one authority to be the best modern church in Worcestershire. Its interior has a mellow quality with exquisite wood and plasterwork in the Art Nouveau style. This was carried out by the Bromsgrove Guild which was an art and crafts movement prominent at the beginning of this century.

Dodford still has its school founded in 1877, but like many village schools of a similar size, it struggles to survive. It now takes children up to the age of 9. Most of the village children attend and receive an excellent beginning to their education.

In the 1950s one of the larger houses in the village was adapted as a holiday home for young children from some of Birmingham's deprived or broken homes. Many generous people from far and near have contributed towards its upkeep and it is run by a committee of dedicated volunteers and the warden and her family.

Because of the way it was planned, Dodford has no real centre, no village green; the school is at one end and the pub at the other. In one of the cottages there is a small village shop and post office. Like many villages on the edge of Birmingham, Dodford now has a large proportion of its population of about 650 who are retired or who commute to work in the city. The village was saved from extinction in the late 19th century by strawberry growing, and in the mid-20th century the 'Austin' at Longbridge provided employment for several of the inhabitants. This still continues today although there is now a greater variety of occupations.

Drakes Broughton ✺

In 1857 the Rev Richard Williamson D. D., vicar of Pershore founded a chapel of ease for the benefit of the inhabitants of the then small community of Drakes Broughton. The structure was completed within a few years by the addition of a vestry and wooden steeple. The church came near to national fame when, on the night of 23rd/24th December 1977 the steeple was blown over in a fierce gale. The parishioners succeeded in raising the £11,000 required for its replacement in exactly one year.

St Barnabas school was built in 1891 for 80 children. Before the advent of school buses pupils walked from Wadborough carrying satchels containing all their requirements for the day, including packed lunches. They of course had to walk back home after lessons in the afternoon. After the closure of Stoulton School, pupils from there were transferred to St Barnabas.

In 1954 a fund for a village hall was started with £75 left over from the Coronation celebrations in 1953. For the next five years annual ox roasts and flower shows were held in addition to other money raising events, and the village hall was opened on 12th November 1958.

Prior to 1958 having no village hall was a handicap but not an impossibility. If someone wanted to organize any indoor event it had to be held in St Barnabas School. This was a major upheaval. Heavy desks had to be removed and as the village had no electricity until 1949, hanging paraffin lamps had to be trimmed and water heated on coal fires for beverages!

Traditional local occupations were mainly animal and fruit farming and market gardening. It was a common occurrence to see horse-drawn vehicles taking their produce to Pershore market and the drovers with sheep and cattle bound for Worcester market. Among the resident craftsmen the village could boast a blacksmith, a miller, a shoemaker, a thatcher and a wheelwright. Villagers were also fortunate in having the services of a resident District Nurse, and of course the convenience of a local post office.

There were brickworks in Brickyard Lane and a family of builders known as 'The Kid Glove Builders' because of their perfection, also lived in the village. In 1841 the blacksmith's shop was situated on the main Pershore to Worcester road, not far from Turnpike House, which stood on the corner of Stonebow Road and Worcester Road.

Turnpike House, a well known landmark, was demolished in about 1956/57. In the late 19th century and early 20th century the blacksmith lived and worked at 'The Old Forge' in Mill Lane. Farther down the lane the Old Flour Mill still stands where the blacksmith's craft has now been revived.

It is a great pity that in view of recent development causing the loss of much woodland and many a beauty spot, Drakes Broughton is slowly losing its identity as a village.

Earl's Croome 🌿

Earl's Croome is a small village in south Worcestershire, so small that it is not found on every map. It is reached by the A38, south of Worcester and if you should miss the left turn, sign-posted Earl's Croome and go speeding on past you may say 'Crumbs, was that Earl's Croome?' and you would be quite near the truth because an early name for this parish was Crumba! The name was later changed to Earl's Croome because the patronage of the church came into the possession of the Earls of Warwick in 1369. As late as 1855 no one was quite sure how to spell it and it appears as Iriliscome alias Earl's Croome. Can the Worcestershire speech have had something to do with it?

It would be better to describe this little place as a parish rather than a village, for the parish boundaries take in some scattered farms as well as the houses that lie to the left and right of the A38. There are a few old houses, notably Earl's Croome Court opposite the church which dates from the 17th century as does Woodleys, a farmhouse on the left on the road leading to Pershore via Dunstall Common. The Rectory, Earl's Croome House, and Levant Lodge are 18th century houses. There has been quite a lot of building this century, especially the two pleasant developments on either side of Quay Lane.

The population has changed very little. In 1564 it was 164 and in 1981 was 181, but whereas in the 18th century the men were mostly classed as labourers, in 1950 from a group of seven in the parish register only one was listed as an agricultural worker. The farms still flourish but with a much reduced workforce and most people go out of the village to work. There is one new industrial building near the village hall.

The church of St Nicholas is the most interesting feature of the village, historically speaking. It dates from the 12th century. Earl's Croome church is a favourite place for weddings and when one goes inside it is easy to see why. It is very well proportioned and has a welcoming well-used atmosphere. There are many interesting features, the chancel arch, a 16th century pulpit with linenfold carving, traces of pre-Reformation painting on the window next to it and in the chancel, a loophole window in the east wall and another in the north wall of 12th century origin.

It is rather sad that the school is now closed. It was built in the 19th century. In 1875 the number on roll was 53. It was closed in 1981 and children now go to school in Upton. The post office is also closed, and when the rector retired in 1983 the living was joined with Ripple. There is still quite a lot going on in the village however.

There are lots of walks around Earl's Croome and with its proximity to the river Severn and Dunstall Common nearby, is an ideal picnicking place (lovely views of the Malverns from here). It is a good spot to visit.

Eckington 🌿

In Saxon times a chieftain, named Ecci, together with his retainers (ing) and palisade (tun) produced the name Eckington for this village on the western slopes of Bredon Hill.

The river Avon flows nearby. It could be crossed on foot at one point, and was the route taken by monks travelling between the abbeys at Pershore and Tewkesbury. There is still Pass Street in the village, along which they passed on their pilgrimage. There was a ferry boat crossing, but in 1440 a bridge was built. However, by 1720 repairs were no longer feasible, so the parish paid for the stone bridge which still stands today. It cost £170, plus £20 provided by the county.

Holy Trinity church in the main street dates from the 13th century, and contains a fine Jacobean monument to John Hanford, who built Woollas Hall, which stands 400 feet up on Bredon Hill behind the village. In the churchyard there is a poignant little epitaph on a tombstone:

> Our Earthly Friends They were but few
> God Bless Our Children and the World Adieu.

The village is part of the Vale of Evesham, fruit orchards, farming, market gardens, and, in time past, osier growers, make up the livelihood of many villagers. Self-employed and commuters are plentiful, particularly so when the railway came and the village station was busy and thriving. Sadly, the Beeching Axe fell on Eckington, and now the trains only flash by.

They are fortunate to have a village school, shops, and inns; but the six private schools, the keeper of the stocks, the Pound Piece for straying cattle, and the Eckington Bees are village history. The bees lived in thatched hives and when a member of the beekeeper's family died, a visit had to be made to the hives to tell the bees of the death to prevent them from swarming.

Eckington is one of the necklet of hamlets and villages which circle Bredon Hill, a lovely area at all times of the year, but locals keep their weather eyes open, and remember the old rhyme:

> When Bredon Hill puts on its hat
> Ye men of the Vale beware of that.

Eldersfield

The parish of Eldersfield formed part of what was known as Malvern Chase – a forest which stretched from the Malvern Hills to the river Severn, and is situated on the extreme end of Worcestershire adjoining Staunton, Chaceley and Forthampton which are in Gloucestershire. It is a scattered parish with the church at the north end, and the houses border the narrow roads leading to it. At the south end is Corse Lawn Common stretching about 2 miles in length, with the road from Gloucester to Upton-on-Severn running through it. Here lying off the road are small farms and cottages, many of them having what are known as 'Pastures' – meaning that they are allowed to graze so many sheep and cattle on the Common but which have to be taken in at night. On the Common also is

Eldersfield Lawn school which has a chancel attached and where services are held in conjunction with the main church of St John the Baptist. Eldersfield church is a beautiful one and very old, dating from the 12th century with a perfect Norman arch leading to the chancel. It has a very tall spire and a grand peal of bells, and on the old stone font is the coat of arms of Dick Whittington who held land nearby.

Below the church the road leads to another large open space known as Eldersfield Marsh where in the old days sports and archery took place.

Upon one of the small hills beyond the church lived a herbalist who was known as 'Mary of Eldersfield', and who collected all kinds of herbs for her medicaments. Because she was so good at healing, she was also hunted by doubters who called her 'the witch of Eldersfield' and would have killed her.

Though without shops or post office in its rural situation, Eldersfield is much favoured by picnickers on the Common and there are two public houses, a large hotel and restaurant, two cricket teams, a Women's Institute, and a bus service.

No new houses are allowed to be built on the Common under the Worcestershire County Structure Plan, though nearly all the older houses have been refurbished and brought up to date.

Elmley Castle ✎

The quiet picturesque village of Elmley Castle nestles beneath the northern slopes of Bredon Hill. The village can be approached from Pershore, Evesham and Ashton-under-Hill. The broad main street leads up to a village square surrounded by black and white cottages, beyond which is the church and Bredon Hill.

The village derives its name from the ancient castle which was built during Norman times on a spur of the hill overlooking the village. The castle survived for about 200 years but by the early 1400s was already in ruins. Very little remains of the castle now because over the centuries the stones have been brought down and used in extensions to the church, garden walls and some say even the old bridge over the Avon at Pershore.

During the reign of Henry VIII the Savage family became Lords of the Manor of Elmley and they built their mansion behind the church. Nowadays a modern housing estate stands in the grounds to the front of the original site of the old house.

The attractive Norman church is dedicated to St Mary and has several interesting features. Its outward appearance is of a fortified tower and battlements. Inside is a 12th century carved stone font and an exquisite alabaster memorial to the Savage family. In the churchyard to the front of the church are two unusual sundials dating from the 16th century, one of which depicts the Savage coat of arms.

The village school was built in 1869 and every year the children celebrate Oak Apple Day (the restoration of Charles II to the throne of England) with traditional Maypole Dancing in the village square. On Spring Bank Holiday Monday the WI hold a wayside stall upholding an ancient right to a market stall as decreed in the Magna Carta.

There are three pubs in Elmley. The famous old cider house, The Plough, where cider is made on the premises and sold in the bar. The Queen Elizabeth or 'The Queens' as it is called, which was used for accommodation at the time of a visit of Elizabeth I is an old black and white building with flagstones in the bar and where real ale is served. The third pub is the Old Mill Inn which is tucked away at the far corner of the cricket ground. From the garden you can watch the cricket and have unrivalled views of the church and hill. The mill pond lies behind the pub and although the mill wheel is no longer in place it is interesting to visit and feed the water birds.

Many visitors come to Elmley to walk on Bredon Hill. There are two easily accessible paths onto the hill, one is from the top of Hill Lane and the other is The Wychavon Way which passes close to the village.

There are many old families in Elmley and most are connected by marriage, but also there are newcomers, who have chosen to live here because of the beauty of the surrounding countryside and the quality of life. There are plenty of social activities. The occupations of the people who live in the village are many and various. A number are connected with market gardening and farming, and many commute to work. A number of older people have chosen to retire here, enjoy life in Elmley and help the village community in many ways.

Fairfield ❧

Fairfield is a sprawling village, situated on fairly high ground, about three miles from Bromsgrove, and in Domesday times was part of the great Forest of Feckenham.

Geographically, the nucleus is centred on the Stourbridge Road. Here stands the combined post office, general stores and butcher's shop, and next door is the garage and petrol station.

On the opposite side of the road, behind the War Memorial, looms the village hall. Residents are proud of this fine building, which was erected six years ago, thus replacing the old wooden hall. This venue is the centre of much activity, and accommodates the stalwart WI, going strong for 50 years, a lively drama group of 36 years standing, other clubs catering for the young, the middle-aged and elderly, and of course various church functions.

St Mark's, built 1860, is next to the hall, and is a small, pleasant, well maintained church.

Above the church lies the recreation ground, endowed with swings and seesaws for the youngsters, and a football pitch belonging to an excellent local team.

Fairfield can boast of a farm dating 1669, but alas, its famous arched barn has been converted into retirement flats. The one really large house is Fairfield Court, a 17th century stone house with a timber-framed part dating back to the 16th century.

This is one of the border villages, between the nail-making of Bromsgrove, and the glass-making of Stourbridge. These cottage industries were carried on well into the first part of the 20th century. A nail-making cottage and a glass-making cottage can still be found cheek by jowl! Many interesting anecdotes have been passed on by the older generation.

Now there are many commuters who travel to the city of Birmingham (16 miles away). Nevertheless, the hub of local activity remains strong, even if not so closely knit as in the olden days. The rich essence of living, with its joys and sorrows, are enacted here in a similar way to that of any other small community.

People sometimes call it a prosaic village! Then they lift up their eyes to the distant outline of the Lickey Hills, witness the magical changing of the four seasons, and realise with a glad heart, that this is a good place in which to live.

Far Forest

Far Forest is a small village situated on the edge of Wyre Forest and part of the much larger parish of Rock. There are two churches, one Church of England Holy Trinity and one Baptist, a school, village hall, two shops, one with a post office, and a public house called The Plough Inn.

The early inhabitants were thought to be a godless lot as couples used to live in common-law relationships. A vicar from nearby Ribbesford, in the year 1844, formed a committee and the church was built. A joint of meat was given to all those who regularised their relationship. It was not until 1864 that the church was licenced for baptisms, burials or marriages. All burials were carried out at Ribbesford some three miles away. The coffins had to be carried and the bearers called for sustenance at the various ale houses on the way, namely, The Wheatsheaf, The Plough Inn, The Blue Ball, (The Red Cow) or Green Dragon, The Royal Forester, The New Inn, Mopsons Cross, The Duke William, (Harvatts Place) or Tower Farm, The Running Horse and The Rose and Crown. It is said that by the time the burial party arrived the deceased was in a better condition than the bearers!

The ground for the village hall was given to the village by the Betts family. The hall was built by public subscription in 1932. Over the years it has had a few modifications and is well used by local groups.

A school has been in the village since 1829. The original building is now run by the church as an adventure centre for the benefit of various organisations throughout the country. The new school was built in 1902 by the Rev William Lea, in memory of his parents. When the children reach the age of nine they transfer to Bewdley Middle and then to Bewdley High School. The schools are four miles away and the children are collected and taken by coach.

Industries in the area used to be charcoal burning, forestry, timber felling, farming, and basket making. The railway and the Elan Valley waterpipe line brought many jobs to the area at the turn of the century. Today the railway no longer runs through the forest and although the Elan pipeline is still in use for the Birmingham people, water is now pumped to the village from the Trimpley reservoir. These days most of the inhabitants commute to nearby towns to work. The surviving crafts being farming, rustic work and holly wreath making.

The forest which covers approximately 6,000 acres is mostly owned by the Forestry Commission. Apart from harvesting timber the forest is widely used for recreational purposes. It is famous for the Whitty Pear or Sorb Tree, and has unique flora and fauna. Dr N. E. Hicken of Bewdley has written many books on the subject of the forest.

Finally, Foresters do not live in or at Far Forest but 'on the Forest'!

Feckenham 🦢

Covering 200 miles and taking in 60 villages and hamlets, the great royal Forest in which King John once enjoyed hunting and which took its name from Feckenham has long since disappeared. The thriving football teams which give enjoyment to the locals today play their sport on a recreation field, central to the village, which was once the site of a royal hunting lodge.

Feckenham is more fortunate than many Worcestershire villages insofar as it has mostly escaped the attentions of builders, due to a tight planning policy by the borough council of Redditch. Architecturally the village is a unique mix of building styles; red brick, whitewashed, and half-timbered, with a wealth of fine Georgian dwellings.

Beside football, other activities include a cricket club with an enviable ground and pavilion, badminton, WI and a thriving youth club. The village hall, although handicapped by its somewhat confined sited, enjoys regular bookings and every Saturday evening 'eyes down, look in' signals the start of another bingo session.

The parish church of St John the Baptist still bears witness to its Norman origins and among its treasures are a medieval iron-bound chest fashioned from a single tree trunk, and two fine old oak tables belonging to the historic Blue Coat School which, although it no longer functions as a school, is still a charity which disburses grants to Feckenham students who aspire to higher education. The 13th century tower houses bells, which, from the early 17th century have, at different stages, been augmented to today's fine ring of eight. A devoted band of ringers ensure that they regularly summon worshippers to divine services and the church is also justifiably proud of its choir. The old horse chestnut tree, adjacent to the north side of the tower, is today a forlorn ghost of its once majestic self since a gale, some years ago, snapped the massive iron chains which bound its three great limbs together. In the ensuing mayhem of falling branches the iron railing-surrounded grave of Phoebe Lee, legendary queen of the gipsies who was laid to rest over a century ago, miraculously escaped damage.

Although it is increasingly becoming a dormitory village with properties much sought after by commuters to Redditch, Birmingham and beyond, Feckenham was once quite a centre of the needle industry. A former factory opposite the village green is now a most attractive private dwelling with distinctive semi-circular windows and the stream which meanders to the west supported two watermills engaged in the scouring of the products.

In living memory the village boasted four pubs and ten shops and in the horse-drawn age the Old Black Boy on the Droitwich road served as a staging post. Sadly only one shop and two pubs have survived, although a large leisure stores has taken the place of the little saddlery and fishing tackle shop in what is quaintly known by the old timers as 'Bug Town' immediately outside the village on the Astwood Bank road. Escaping by the skin of its teeth from closure in the interests of 'economy' the local C of E school is once more secure for the time being with a roll of over 50 pupils, and thus, instead of being lost for ever, it still plays its important role of binding the community together, and is increasingly finding favour with parents from outside.

Finstall ❧

Finstall, meaning a place for heaping wood, was part of Feckenham Forest, where wood was cut for use in the Salt Works at Stoke. There would probably have been a two-way traffic of wood and salt from one area to the other. It was also part of Stoke Manor, which was given to the Church of Worcester, and included a Priory, so the monks would also go along the forest paths on their travels.

Sandstone is to be found in many places, and the remains of old quarries still exist. The older houses in the village are built from this stone, also walls and bridges.

Finstall was on the old coaching road to London, and was a changing place for passengers and horses. The railway was built in 1840, and the section through Finstall is part of the Lickey Incline, which was famous for its steam engine, built in 1919, and nick-named 'Big Bertha'. This engine was used to assist the freight trains up the line to Blackwell.

The site of the old chapel of St Godwald is alongside the railway, and although the chapel was listed as a building of special architectural or historic interest, an order was granted in 1969 permitting its demolition. The National School, built in 1848, was opposite the chapel but it is now a private dwelling. The new church of St Godwald and the school were built on the other side of the railway in the Aston Fields part of the parish. Not far from the churchyard is the Gospel Hall, and over the road the Bromsgrove Rugby Club have found a home on part of Finstall Park. The house itself was at one time a boys preparatory school.

With the coming of the railway, there was easy access to Birmingham, so many prominent business men occupied the big houses – a fore-runner of todays commuters? For over 50 years there was a stud farm, with a high reputation for blood stock, but a lot of this land has now been taken over by housing. The village was known as a healthy place to live, probably because, between 1895 and 1900, no less than three people lived to be 100 or over – a good enough reputation for those days.

The village hall was built by the Albright family and opened in 1904 as a place for social, educational, religious, and recreational activities. There was a fire a few years later, which partially destroyed the building, but this was put right, and in 1936 the ownership of the hall was handed over to trustees by Miss Maria Catherine Albright, and run by a Management Committee. The hall is still being run successfully with the same aims in view.

Inhabitants can still be served at the Cross Inn (probably dating originally from the 17th century), the post office and shop, a shop now making and selling soft furnishings, a nursery for plants, a hotel restaurant (which was originally Finstall Mount), and a kennels. Although Finstall is not as rural as it was, land having been taken up by the railway, houses, and the new Redditch Road, farming is still carried on.

Fladbury

On cold winter days scuttling through the village, one can easily forget the one thing, more than any other, that has influenced the development of Fladbury. But after a few days of heavy rain one can hear the thunderous roar of water rushing over the weir and see flood water creeping over the road at the bottom of Mill Bank; the river Avon once more making its presence felt. For although the village is built along the river's west bank there are only two public places to get to the water's edge; the rest is hidden by church, houses and trees. Balmy summer days provide the impetus to wander down by Ferry Cottage, where the ferry now lies submerged but visible, amongst the reeds, yellow water iris and king-cups. The strong cable still stretches across the river to the island where Cropthorne Mill stands. Back onto the road and a few yards down is a grassed area owned by the village called the 'coal wharf' where one can sit and watch the weir by Fladbury Mill.

The first record of Fledanburg, 'town by the river' or 'protected town of the flood lands', was in AD 691 when Ethelred, King of Mercia gave it to Ofter, Bishop of Worcester, for the use of the monks already living there. The monks have long gone, but a monastery now in private hands remains in the centre of the village opposite the church.

Until 1887 when the Jubilee Bridge was built there was only one road into the village and a gated track out, down the mill bank across the flat meadows to where it was possible to ford the river.

Cropthorne and Fladbury mills worked closely together for centuries grinding flour and making cider. In 1635 Mr W Sandys who then owned Fladbury mill used £20,000 of his own money to make the river from Tewkesbury to Stratford-upon-Avon navigable so that it was then possible to bring much-needed coal up-river and take produce including 'withies' out. In 1899 Fladbury 'saw the light' when the Fladbury Electric Light and Power Company was formed at the mill and the village became one of the first to have electric street lighting. Power was also supplied to private houses at the rate of 'A penny per night, per light, per-haps!'. Although Fladbury mill worked into the 20th century both mills are now private residences.

The fertile river terraces were excellent for agriculture and the river meadows were control-flooded very early in the year to warm the soil to get early grass for cattle. Until well after the Second World War the majority of people living in the village worked on the land, some on large farms but many families grew market garden produce on small plots of land in the village itself. Every day cart loads of fresh vegetables and plums in season would be loaded on goods waggons in the railway siding to be delivered next morning to markets all over England, Scotland and Wales.

The village today retains many of its fine old buildings and quaint alley-ways, but it is a developing village with the river again an influence, this time for leisure, with private boats, hired pleasure boats using Fladbury lock, canoeing and of course fishing. As long as the Avon flows Fladbury will remain.

Flyford Flavel

A compact village on a hill with an inn, The Boot, a modern shop and the church.

Flavel was the name of a Norman family.

At the bottom of the hill on the A422 road is another inn, called the Union, said to be at the extremes of three parishes.

Nearby is Grafton Flyford, a pleasant rural area with a church and an old school, now a village hall. The name means a settlement in the forest, and Flyford is the trackway through 'frithe' (forest).

The church of St John the Baptist is mostly 19th century with the original 14th century tower.

Frankley 🌿

The ancient parish of Frankley with its beautiful 12th century church is only a mile or two from the centre of Halesowen and adjoins its eastern boundary. Frankley is best known today for its beeches on the hill which provide a landmark that can be seen from many parts of the Black Country area.

The manor of Frankley came into the possession of the Lyttleton family during the 13th century. A splendid moated manor house was erected, the site of which can still be seen in the lane leading to the church. In the 15th century, the house was the home of the famous English Justice of the Common Pleas, Sir Thomas Lyttleton. He had a pool constructed near the house based on the dimensions of Westminster Hall to remind him of that illustrious place. The pool was filled in, but Westminster Farm is still there to remind us of a famous man of law. In 1645, shortly before the battle of Naseby, the manor house was destroyed by Prince Rupert to prevent it being taken and used as a Parliamentary garrison.

Today the pride of Frankley is the church of St Leonard. Little is known of its origins but there is evidence to believe that it dates from the 12th or early 13th century. A much needed restoration was carried out in 1873. A great tragedy struck the church on the night of 9th March 1931 when a disastrous fire completely gutted the tower and organ and caused extensive damage to the nave. The Birmingham Fire Brigade was called but the church lay some 200 yards outside the city boundary and therefore was beyond their responsibilities. The blaze was finally fought by the Bromsgrove Brigade. The church was restored, only to be gutted by fire again in 1947.

Today St Leonard's is in a remarkably good state of repair and bears testimony to the care exercised over hundreds of years to preserve this ancient church.

Great Comberton ✺

Great Comberton is of Saxon origin, when it was a parish of some 965 acres and the settlement of the Cumbra family. In the 13th century it was known as Magna Cumbritune. The village has remained, as one observer put it, 'strikingly pretty on a slope of Bredon Hill bounded by the Avon', and so far controlled development has melded with the renovation of the black and white cottages. The most immediate impact on the visitor is made by the tower of St Michael's church and the total lack of a shop or pub.

In Norman times the owners of the parish provided a very basic way of life (sheep grazing, corn growing, fishing etc), and this kept the population at around 200 with Pershore as the market town. This pattern exists today since the nearest shops and amenities are in Pershore. The site of the village landing-stage can still be reached via Quay Lane. This was where corn was loaded onto boats to be taken down to Nafford Mill. There is also a record of fisheries in 1298.

There are several black and white thatched cottages dating back to the time of Queen Elizabeth I. Many of these were built with timbers from cottages of an even earlier date. Bank Cottage was the home of the Whoods family for 300 years. They were the village food suppliers and baked bread in what is now the sitting room of the modernised cottage.

In the 19th century fruit orchards predominated following the introduction of improved apple and pear stock and the Pershore plum. An entry from a household diary reads: '... made 12lbs Pershore plum jam and 13 gallons of wine'.

Rebuilding of the church is attributed to the manorial Beauchamps of Elmley Castle (c1300), and it was noted that all burials up to the year 1510 had to be made in the precincts of the powerful Pershore Abbey which collected the required revenues. The most prominent memorial in the churchyard is the column erected by members of a volunteer fire brigade in Sydney, Australia, in memory of Edmund Smith, their captain, who had once lived in Great Comberton and who was drowned on his return to England when the *Royal Charter* was wrecked in 1859 off the coast of Anglesey.

Across a field from the church stands the house built by the grandfather of John Masefield the poet, Reverend Parker, who was the rector of St Michael's from 1826 to 1864. John Masefield was a frequent visitor to the village.

The present population of over 300 has increased little over the years. The village has two farms and a market garden. Some of the inhabitants commute to outlying towns as far as Birmingham. In the summer of 1940 the Women's Institute held a Flower Show which gradually grew over the years until the village took it over as an annual event. It is held on August Bank Holiday Saturday and is well supported, even drawing people from the industrial Midlands.

Great Comberton has not yet been spoilt and hopefully will remain a quiet English country village for many years to come.

Great Witley

Great Witley is best approached via the A443 from Worcester, from which a delightful view unfolds of the village as it nestles below the hardwood clad Abberley Hills and the largely conifered slopes of Woodbury Hill.

The striking Hundred House, with its origins in the 18th century, is worthy of special mention. It was the centre for many events in the social calendar with stock sales on adjoining land, still known as the Sale Yard. It housed the court room and cell accommodation and was so used until the present police station and court house were built in 1872.

The main attraction of Great Witley these days is the ruin of Witley Court, now cared for by English Heritage, and the adjacent nationally famous, unique parish church, both of which attract tens of thousands of visitors throughout the year.

The origins of Witley Manor date back to the 13th century but it was not untill 1655 that the manorial rights of six manors – 2600 acres in all – were consolidated by Thomas Foley, the first of six generations of ironmasters from the Black Country. The Court, which they built during the years 1655–1837, was then to become the home of the Dudley family who came to own over 9,000 acres in the parish of Great Witley and the adjoining parishes. The Dudleys added further extensions and embellishments to the house before selling it to Sir Herbert Smith, a Kidderminster carpet manufacturer in 1920. His occupancy terminated with a disastrous fire in 1937. Life in the village during this long period revolved around its associations with the Court.

From 1843 – 1846 the Court was tenanted by Queen Adelaide following the death of her husband William IV. Her quiet concern for the village was demonstrated in the building of the original school with

76

accommodation for two teaching staff. This attractive building on the Worcester Road is at present used as the village hall, as a 'new' school was built in 1895 almost opposite the original school. This flourishing school with about 120 pupils and 5 teaching staff, now serves several of the surrounding villages whose smaller schools were forced to close.

Witley Court had its heyday in the period of the Dudley occupancy when Edward VII and other notable society figures were frequent visitors availing themselves of the extensive sporting facilities – bags of over a thousand head of game were commonplace – and enjoying the lavish hospitality which provided the basis for many tales, remembered to this day, for the extravagance and ostentation.

The cemetery chapel and burial ground, alongside the Worcester Road, was given to the village by Lord Dudley in 1882. The chapel is now used as a headquarters for the local Scouts and Guides.

The present parish church replaced a medieval church on almost the same site. Started by Lady Foley in 1733, and probably designed by James Gibbs, the church was built adjacent to Witley Court and with direct access to it. The 2nd Baron Foley wished to embellish the church and it was transformed into its present baroque splendour. Miraculously, the church remained untouched by the fire which led to the devastation of the Court.

One further very different event placed Great Witley on the map early in the present century and is vividly recalled by older inhabitants. Every Easter Monday for some 40 years motor cyclists from far and wide gathered to compete in the 'freak' hill climb up the precipitous face of Abberley Hill. The village was virtually taken over by the enthusiastic spectators and the competitors who roared their way up and back down the hill again.

Today, the parish is set in a farming community with arable, dairy, sheep and fruit farming predominating. With its easy access to neighbouring towns, the village provides a focus for those wanting to enjoy the scenery of the Teme valley as well as many pleasant walks to tempt the rambler. Like so many other rural villages, the beautiful setting attracts today's mobile commuting public, members of which have converted and modernised many of the houses which once provided homes for the employees of earlier wealthy landowners.

Grimley ✍

Grimley is a large, widespread parish, about 4½ miles north of Worcester, with Grimley Brook roughly forming its northern boundary.

The church, school and post office are all in the north-east corner, in what is known as Grimley Village, which straggles along the village street from the Wagon Wheel Inn at one end, to the Camp House Inn, a pleasant old hostelry on the banks of the Severn at the other.

About 1½ miles due west, past the large old vicarage, is Sinton Green, where the parish hall is situated; the scene of many local activities. Here there also used to be a post office and village shop, which alas closed down and is now a hairdresser's.

About a mile further west from Sinton Green we come to Monkwood, one of the oldest woods in the country, going back thousands of years, and of great botanical and wildlife interest. It was recently purchased by the Worcestershire Conservation Trust. At Monkwood Green, also a haunt of botanists and entomologists, is the western extremity of the parish.

A quarter of a mile south of Sinton Green is another hamlet, on the southern boundary, aptly named Worlds End – a good place to end this brief geographical tour.

The present parish church, dating back to the Normans, is dedicated to St Bartholomew and celebrated its 800th anniversary in 1979. The tower was rebuilt in 1845 and it was then that the unusual porch in Norman style was set up, with an arcaded outside stairway leading up to the gallery. There is a ring of six bells, the tenor bell being the oldest cast in a Worcester medieval foundry in 1482.

In the churchyard stands an ancient preaching cross, listed as being of great historical interest and protected by the Department of the Environment. A few yards away is the tomb in which lie the ashes of that intrepid Victorian explorer, Samuel White Baker. He lived for a time in Elm Hill, a grand old house with a beautiful view over village and riverside. Napoleon Bonaparte's younger brother, Lucien, lived in the great house called Thorngrove during the time of the Napoleonic Wars.

Around the turn of the 19th century the parish must have been a bustling thriving community. On Sinton Green there was a forge and a wheelwright, as well as the post office and stores. Between Sinton Green and Grimley Village was Ball Mill where there was, obviously, a mill with a bakery, and a butcher next door. The mill used the water of

Grimley Brook as late as the 1930s to generate electricity for the bakery and for Thorngrove house.

Many people worked on the farms, there was a lot of glove-making going on as a cottage industry, and a brickworks on the river's edge provided work for some more people. One elderly inhabitant remembers that his grandfather worked there as a boy, treading the clay with his bare feet. Of course, taking the clay out of the ground created the osier beds and swamps all along the river.

Today the main industry in the parish is Ball Mill Sand & Gravel. The sand gained from the Severn Terraces is of top quality and much sought after by the building industry. Several smaller firms provide some work, but, as is now generally the custom, most villagers work elsewhere.

Guarlford ❧

Guarlford as a parish is quite modern, only about 150 years old, but the district has been inhabited since pre-Roman days. Through medieval times Guarlford was a demesne manor of Great Malvern Priory, and with about 360 acres under the plough must have been a busy place.

In Victorian days it was considered necessary to build a chapel of ease near the old manor house of Guarlford Court to serve this more distant part of the Malvern domain and in 1843 Lady Emily Foley laid the foundation stone. A few years later it became the church of a new and separate parish. Soon a rectory was built and a school between, so the scattered village had a centre.

The main feature of the village is the road running almost straight across the parish except for an 'S' bend near the church, and bordered by wide verges, remnants of Malvern Chase.

An old Malt House stands near the church. The last maltster departed about the time of the First World War, and it became a village possession. Part of the building was then used as a Men's Club, open four evenings a week, with a bar and a billiards table in the tower room. The large upper floor has been in use as a village hall ever since.

In those days almost all the village population were engaged in agriculture and it was practically self-supporting. There was a baker in Chance Lane who was one of the last to use the old stick oven, two village shops, one selling sweets and cigarettes, the other everything from paraffin to whipping tops, two public houses, three blacksmiths, a wheelwright, a coffin-maker, and several basket makers at Clevelode. A grocer from Malvern delivered regularly in a horse-drawn van, as did a butcher from Upton-on-Severn in a very smart butcher's cart, driven by a man in a spotless white coat and blue-striped apron. On other occasions he was found leading the band for the dances in the village hall.

During the war, a man was working in the fields at Guarlford Court when an aircraft crashed nearby. He pulled the navigator to safety but the unconcious pilot was trapped in his seat. Ignoring the exploding ammunition the man managed to wrench the seat out and carried the pilot, still strapped to his seat, to the safety of a ditch seconds before the plane blew up. For this he was awarded the George Medal.

The post-war years have seen great changes. Whereas before most people travelled by bicycle or pony and trap, the car now enabled them to go farther afield for entertainment. Some farms were absorbed by larger units, the old farmhouses becoming private residences, and the others, being mechanised and with the help of modern technology, were run mainly by the farmer and his family.

The school closed and the younger children travel by bus to a neighbouring village, the older ones to Malvern. The Rectory too is now a private house and the parish shares a priest with two other villages. Three small pleasant housing estates provide homes for people whose work is outside the village.

Hallow 🦩

Rushing along the A443 Worcester to Tenbury road, as most traffic does, you could get a false impression of Hallow as it flashes past. To discover the interesting features you should stop awhile, leave the car, and explore on foot the many lanes and paths leading from either side of the main road which cuts through the centre of the village.

In the Domesday Book the village appears as Haleghan. This comes from a word meaning a hill, or rising ground, and the original settlements would have been on land rising up from the riverside. Footpaths from the village lead down to the river Severn, an important communication link in the early days, but not really part of village life now.

There has been a school in the village since the beginning of the 18th century, and Hallow CE Primary School is alongside the main road in the centre of the village. The present school was built in 1857 and has a distinctive clock tower.

Snowdrops and crocuses appear in a fine display along the main drive

The Parish Church of St Philip and St James, Hallow

to Hallow Park School each spring, closely followed by many thousands of daffodils at Easter time. In the 16th century Queen Elizabeth I hunted in Hallow Park and visited the manor belonging to the Habington family. The present impressive building with its tall chimneys and ornamental balustrades, was built in 1914 on the site of the Elizabethan manor. Formerly the home of the Banks family, textile millionaires, it was then a Dr Barnardo's Home for many years and now it houses a special school for teenage girls.

The parish church of St Philip and St James with its tall spire is the first landmark when approaching from Worcester. This is the village's third church, built from local sandstone from Holt Quarry in 1869. A tower was added later, but the 150 foot high spire, the peal of eight bells and the clock were dedicated in 1900 by Mrs Charles Wheeley Lea, of the Lea and Perrins family, as a memorial to her late husband. In the old churchyard, some distance away, the grave of Sir Charles Bell can be found. A distinguished surgeon, he is remembered for his work on the nervous system. He was visiting Hallow Park in 1842 when he had a heart attack, and Lord Jeffrey wrote an inscription on a tablet which was placed in the 'new' church.

There are many thriving village organisations meeting regularly at the village hall behind the Crown Inn. The adjoining playing fields and tennis courts host a variety of sporting activities throughout the year, as well as other outdoor functions connected with the church or the village. In spite of the shopping attractions of St Johns and the city centre there remain two shops – a village store and a post office/newsagent, and several garages.

On May Day (the first of May, *not* the Bank Holiday!) a May Queen is crowned on the Village Green. Then, unperturbed by the heavy traffic trundling past, the children dance round the maypole.

Convenient for Worcester – yes; part of suburbia – definitely no! The fiercely independent villagers of Hallow refuse to be swallowed up. They continue to support any legislation which maintains the precious mile of Green Belt which separates them from the city. This determination secures their heritage and ensures their future as part of rural Worcestershire.

Hanbury ❧

Hanbury parish is quite large, but the village itself is centred around the public house, The Vernon Arms, and the corner shop. The school and church are situated about 1½ to 2 miles from the village. The church was built in the 12th century and a monastery may have existed there in the 7th century. The church is still in regular use. There was also a small school at Broughton Green, a hamlet but still in Hanbury parish. This building was also a church, and although the school closed in the 1940s church services were held there until about 1986.

The Squire lived at Hanbury Hall and he owned most of the farms and cottages in Hanbury. The Bearcrofts of Mere Hall owned the farms and cottages in Broughton Green. In the 1920s the children of Broughton Green school were given a Christmas Party and presents by Colonel and Mrs Bearcroft, and in August the children of both schools were given a party at Hanbury Hall by Sir George Vernon, the last Vernon to live there. The children had tea in the Long Gallery (with deer heads adorning the walls) and then races on the extensive lawns – and balloons! These were a kind of miniature air balloon, which were inflated and some kind of liquid (maybe methylated spirit) was poured into the suspended base and then set alight. Unfortunately these balloons never seemed to travel very far, always burning the actual balloon! Hanbury Hall is now a National Trust property, and the Annual Village Fete is usually held in the grounds.

The village hall was then called the Club Room and was used as a Working Men's Club and also used for concerts and by the local Choral Society. The village shop was next to the Vernon Arms and sold groceries, foodstuff for fowls and pigs, paraffin, a little greengrocery (although most people grew their own vegetables), and at weekends pork pies and sausages were on sale. There was no electricity until late 1948, no company water and no main sewer until much later (the 1960s). The Courts Close council houses were first occupied early in 1949. Originally this site was the Pound Field, renowned for mushrooms! Water for taps and toilets was supplied from a borehole close by and pumped to the houses, and a sewerage filter bed and cess pit were situated at one end of the estate. A number of old peoples' bungalows have now been built on the Courts Close Estate, with a Warden on call.

One compound for stock sales was situated in the field where Hanbury Garage now stands. A second compound stood on the Droitwich Road.

Chappell & Foster and Luce & Silvers of Bromsgrove, had a sale each, in spring and autumn. Hanbury Garage was then only a small building adjoining the Vernon Arms.

In the centre of the village a cross stands in a Memorial Garden to the memory of the men of the parish who gave their lives in the two World Wars, and a Roll of Honour hangs in the church.

Hanley Castle

Hanley's castle was built on the orders of King John, probably as a sort of royal hunting lodge, and later in its history passed to the Earl of Warwick. In the 16th century it was the seat of administration of the very severe forest laws that governed Malvern Chase; a deep-sunken road still bears the name Hangman's Lane.

The castle has now gone but the area remains full of black and white cottages and sturdy farms, many hundreds of years old. Merevale Farm is one such. The farm has a ghost, reputed to be a one-eyed bulldog named Charlie by his Royalist owner. When Parliamentarians won at the Battle of Worcester in 1651 the dog was hanged from a large oak tree in the Merevale garden to banish the Royalist connections.

Once the village had a market, a major status symbol which required a royal charter. A busy commercial life was supported by the pottery industry and by the quay on the river Severn which flows and sometimes floods at the bottom of Quay Lane. Quay Lane, today a quiet, sleepy backwater, thinly populated, was once of much more importance. One of the three village inns (now a private house) was situated almost at the bottom of the lane – within living memory its door furniture was in the shape of jugs! – and beside it is a slip of a field where the cattle drovers used to lie up overnight.

The illegitimate son of a woman in the village was born here in 1495, his father thought to be 'a clerke'. Helped by the Lechmere family he received a good education, was an ambassador for Henry VIII, and rose in the church under Cardinal Wolsey to become Bishop of London. He was Bishop Bonner, growing up in Bonner's Cottage, Quay Lane. An interesting architectural detail on the cottage is the 'roof finial', a pottery smoke outlet (this one shaped rather like a pineapple) typical of the Welsh borders; another example in the village is to be seen on the roof of 'Nell's Lounge Bar' at The Three Kings inn by the church.

The river Severn here is thought originally to have been fordable, the water level rising over the years, particularly when there was more widespread canalisation. Floods have always been a feature of Severnside life.

On the occasion of the marriage of Queen Victoria's eldest son, later to be Edward VII, to the beautiful Alexandra of Denmark, three oak trees were planted in the village to commemorate the event. One was planted on Hanley Quay Wharf, one at the Cross Hands, and one on the green of the daughter village of Hanley Swan. This last is now a magnificent and most beautifully shaped specimen, the real essence of 'village green' – but it was not so without some unusual help. A story is handed down from generation to generation in the village that when the young sapling was planted on the green, it took a long time to 'get going' and appeared to be stunted. By chance a travelling circus happened to stay on the green and the story is that an elephant while being exercised leaned over the railings and bit out the top of the young tree. Generations of villagers have maintained ever since that that is why it is such a glorious example and so perfectly shaped!

Hartlebury ✍

It can be said that Hartlebury village stands firmly in the 20th century with its rapidly developing trading estate containing 150 businesses and employing 1,750 people, the largest brickworks in Europe producing 1¼ million bricks each week, and modern farms supplying direct to the community. It has two traditional shops, a post office and a new hairdressing salon serving a community newly expanded to embrace commuters from nearby towns and cities as well as families established here since the Domesday Book was compiled.

At the heart of the village lies the Castle, seat of the Bishops of Worcester, with its famous Hurd Library and State Rooms open to the public and now also housing the County Museum with its collection of gypsy caravans. This fine building, much visited by Royalty in recent years, has long been the centre of village activities, flower shows, fetes and musical events.

St James' parish church, much rebuilt, has a bell dated 1678 and another over 550 years old. Its modern oak pews are carved with the dates and arms of Bishops of Worcester from 680 to 1908. The old Rectory has a splendid classical facade and, with the White Hart, The

Old Bakery and the many charming houses surrounding the church combines to create a tranquil setting at the centre of the village.

The village school built in 1878 was visited by Prince Philip and Bishop Robin Woods on its centenary and is still flourishing. Sadly Queen Elizabeth Grammar School, founded as early as 1472 and given a Royal Charter in 1565, disappeared in July 1977 to be replaced by Bowbrook Private School. The old parish hall was replaced in 1955 by the combined efforts of almost every village inhabitant, raising money, laying foundations, providing labour and building skills. The hall is in constant use by community groups of all kinds.

Hartlebury Common and the river Severn border the village on the western side. The Common is one of the most important inland dune-type habitats in the country and is now a local nature reserve run by the County Council. There are many rare plants including the insectivorous sundew, cotton grass and bog pondweed in the acid bog – the only such site in Worcestershire. This favourite leisure area with walks, bridle paths, picnic places and extensive views towards the Abberley Hills is an added bonus to life in Hartlebury.

Times have changed in Hartlebury; many will say not for the better, but some things remain the same. The ancient Mitre Oak still stands by the side of the main Worcester Road, though today its remaining branches are more likely to be further blighted by the fumes of passing HGVs than to snatch a mitre from the head of a passing Bishop!

Headless Cross 🌿

Headless Cross was not, as some might imagine, a place of execution. It first appears in manuscript in 1275 as Headley, and as late as the early 19th century was written 'Headley's Cross' and could, according to historians, have been the clearing of some Saxon chieftain whose name was Hedda.

The main industry was needle-making. It was a cottage industry, with all the numerous processes carried out by men, women and children. Needlemakers' cottages were recognisable by their windows – very wide in proportion to their height in order to provide light for the minute processes. Some of the needle manufacturers themselves lived in the village. Some of the processes of the fishing tackle industry were also carried out in cottages.

The inhabitants of Headless Cross were a God-fearing people, though the Methodists seemed to have shown greater enterprise than the Anglicans and began worship in 1820 in a house in Birchfield Road. In 1827 they built their first chapel, replacing it in 1858 and again in 1873. This chapel was destroyed in 1873 by an extraordinarily violent gale which caused the building to collapse in a matter of minutes. It is a great tribute to the strength and wealth of the Methodists in the area that they had the existing church built within a year.

The village church, St Luke's (built 1843 and re-built 1867) stands in Evesham Road. Opposite was the village school behind which was the walled, kitchen garden of the Rectory, a rambling Victorian house framed by banks of rhododendrons. The house was approached by a long, wide drive from the road past the 200 year old horse chestnut tree. In spring the ground beneath the tree was bright with snowdrops, crocuses and wild anemones. It was a great joy to walk back from church on Easter morning and enjoy the glorious array of golden daffodils which followed the early spring flowers.

The garden at the back of the house was equally beautiful, with rolling lawns, rustic arches and climbing roses, and the church garden party was quite an event, with dancing on the lawns in the evening to the strains of a silver band. In the daytime teas were served under the old horse chestnut tree, with various stalls, competitions and entertainment by the local schoolchildren. Sadly, with the advent of the New Town of Redditch the bull-dozers took their toll, and in place of all this beauty there now stands what many consider to be a monstrosity of a building housing the telephone exchange.

Two interesting buildings still remain. The Park Inn, which is situated on the site of a former toll house, and the original water tower, erected in 1882 but now obsolete, and replaced by a new water tower of an extraordinary architectural design!

Heightington

The village, which even today consists only of scattered farms and houses, is situated in the north-west corner of Worcestershire, 600 feet above sea level. It lies between the Stourport/Tenbury and the Bewdley/Tenbury roads and was, before the building of the Bewdley bridge in 1447, the main route from the Redstone Ford over the river Severn to Cleobury Mortimer and westwards towards Wales. In early days it was the settlement, 'ton' of the Hyht people.

The church, known as the Chapel of St Giles, is now 20 feet smaller than it was when first built. The earliest record of 1325 shows it as being a chapel of ease in the Wyre Forest and was used as such by King John when he hunted there.

A couple of unusual field names in the area are 'Devil's Bibb' near a hillock called 'Devil's Spadeful' and 'The Lady's Waist'.

The village hall, an ex-army hut of the First World War, was once cold and bleak with no water or electric light. Great efforts were made and the village hall was vastly improved in the 1950s and 1960s, and thanks to the hard work of the present village hall committee it is hoped in the not too distant future a new hall will be built.

On a clear day there is a wonderful view from the rear of the hall when the Abberley Hills, the Malverns, Bredon Hill and the Cotswolds can be seen. At night the lights of Stourport and Worcester show up.

The local telephone exchange, Rock, in the late 1940s was a very friendly affair, manned by a middle-aged lady. For example, if you rang someone up, instead of 'No Reply' she would probably tell you it was useless to ring at that time as she had just seen them getting on the bus to Kidderminster – or they were in the garden and wouldn't hear. Alternatively, if you were expecting a call which hadn't materialised, and you had to go out, she would give a message to the caller telling them when you were likely to be back. It was a great loss to the community when it became automatic!

Himbleton 🦢

In a clearing in the Forest of Feckenham in the reign of King Stephen (1135 – 1154) a church was built. In the next three centuries it was enlarged and a wooden turret added, and became the church we know today in Himbleton.

The school was built in 1874, and between the wars had three teachers, and pupils ranged from 5 to 14 years. Secondary education was available in Worcester for bright scholars who passed an entrance examination. In 1943 education changed and from the age of 11 children were taken by bus to Pershore Secondary Modern School. Now the pupils leave Himbleton at age nine for Middle School at Droitwich. For the past 30 years villagers have periodically fought to keep the school open. At present it still is.

The picturesque black and white pub has had three names during this century, The Harrow (or Arrow) then the Douglas Galton Arms, and now the Galton Arms. It is now an up to date comfortable public house, serving meals and snacks, with clubs for crib, darts etc. Under the same roof was the village shop, which also had a chequered career, from a general store and bakery in the early part of the century, until, alas, it was finally closed. The Plough, licensed for cider only, also sold various household commodities, sweets and cigarettes.

The village butcher collected his meat on Fridays by horse and trap from Worcester, and opened his shop in The Row on Saturdays. He also travelled in winter, by bicycle, around a large area, killing pigs and preparing them for curing into bacon and ham. Next to the butcher's shop, his brother made willow baskets and at the end of The Row was the blacksmith's forge, worked by a second brother, following their father's trade. The Row was transformed some years ago into two houses, and is now one house, called The Old Smithy.

In an old book, Himbleton is described as 'the village of the bindweed on the river Bow'. Bow Brook runs through the village and has always been subject to flooding after much rain. The stream is small in summer, but can become quite a sea, impassable for most traffic except tractors and high vehicles. Some years ago a high flood would last for a week, and there are houses which have had the brook flowing through them. Nowadays a very high flood can rise and then be gone within 12 hours. New residents find their first flood somewhat daunting, but those houses where sandbags were at the ready, have mostly been adapted to be above the water level.

The Midland Red used to run daily bus services, including Sundays and with a late bus on Saturdays, leaving Worcester at 10pm for cinemagoers. Now there is one bus each way on two days a week.

In the past 30 years the village has lost much: policeman, district nurse, resident vicar, the vicarage, post office and shop. There is still the church, school, parish hall, garage and pub, and best of all a good community spirit.

Holdfast

Holdfast, anciently written Holefast, of which the first part of the name means Hollow, alludes to its situation. It is surrounded by Queenhill Bank and the Church hill and is shut off from Longdon by the Long Cover. It nudges Queenhill on the loop from the Longdon to Upton road.

Its parishioners now worship at the church of St Nicholas, Queenhill, but there was a chapel here, situated close by Holdfast Hall. It had no right of burial and was described by Habington (1560–1647) as being so ruined he 'durst look into it, but saw on the North wall a young King riding a red lion'.

Like Queenhill, the river Severn has always played a large part in the community and over the years has claimed many lives. In 1613 a petition was addressed to the Quarter Sessions by hundreds of fishermen of Worcestershire and Shropshire, complaining that the people of Upton, Holdfast and Ripple fished with nets reaching across the river and from top to bottom of it, so that they took all the fish, sometimes 60 salmon at a draught, and the river was destroyed for fishing. Nowadays, the banks are lined with Birmingham Anglers, who own the fishing rights.

There are some good houses. Glebe House is a nice timber-framed building with buttressed wall. The Close was restored in the 1970s. Close Cottage, with its crooked chimney, restored and enlarged a little later, was the sweet shop at the turn of the century. The Forge, opposite, is now a private house.

Holdfast Manor was formerly Barnes House, the Home of an armigerous family (entitled to bear a coat of arms) who intermarried over the centuries with the Knottesfords but, because John Knottesford Barnes predeceased his father by dying at the age of ten, the demise of Thomas Barnes in 1844 ended the line and the house later became known as The Mansion House.

In the early 1900s Hilda Hemus cultivated sweet peas on a farm in the area, called Paradise, and the air was laden with their heady perfume. Local children picked the sweet peas in the evening and, in the morning, the women boxed the blooms in fan-shaped bunches, to be sent up to London on the train from Upton Station. Hilda was so famous for her sweet peas that Edward VII asked that she be presented to him.

In 1863 a young lady by the name of Fanny Baker, living at Southend Farm across the fields, wrote a diary which came to light this century in a Hereford bookshop and is now held in Worcester Library. In it Fanny told of the daily events on the farm and mentioned by name all the people who lived in the district; all those who asked her out to tea, to supper, and to the crowded convivial parties, which went through to breakfast time, at the big houses and in the great cheese barns which are no more.

Today, much of the companionship in this happy community is engendered by Queenhill and District WI whose hall is situated on ground given by the Guilding family, the present owners of Southend Farm.

Holt 🍃

Holt or Holt Castle, as the village was called in medieval times, is a Saxon word meaning 'wood', and it is thought that the wood which today stands on the high ground to the south of St Martin's church, gave the village its name. A few yards from the church is impressive Holt Castle, both buildings being part Norman in origin, dating from the 11th century and built of local sandstone. Many titled families have lived in the castle.

The village grew up around the castle and church, and at the time of the Conquest the population was 24. Today it is around 600. The village of those early days has long since vanished and now the church and castle and a few cottages form a small hamlet, while the village has grown either side of the main road, a third of a mile away. This area was originally called the Heath and for many years now this part of the village has been known as Holt Heath. There were some farm cottages and some pre-war council houses, now demolished and replaced by a smart council estate and two more recent private estates, all exceptionally well laid out.

Until latter years, Holt had a police station and a village school, neither of which exist today. Holt children now go by coach to Grimley and then at 11 years on to the Chantry High at Martley. There are two public houses, the Fleet Hotel by the riverside and the Red Lion Inn. Perhaps the most important building, the heart and hub of the village, is the 'Hall', built in 1930 and used by a local operatic society, activity group for under 11s, bingo, whist drives and the Women's Institute.

Holt has another claim to fame, Broomfield's Farm Shop. Adjoining the shop are Broomfield's apple orchards, which are so neat and well cared for. The apples are picked, graded and sold in the shop, along with other produce.

The land and the farming industry has changed drastically, more so in the post-war years. Pre-war there were hopyards, cherry, apple and plum orchards and market gardening, and most of the inhabitants worked in the fields. Now only a few people are employed on the farms. Some local housewives pick and grade apples, and the travelling caravan dwellers pick the sprouts, etc. Most others commute to the nearby towns. Many acres of prime agricultural ground and apple orchards sadly had to make way for sand and gravel but happily as the machinery moves to the next patch, the emptied ground is being put back to grass, with some groupings of trees. The large pools resulting from the gravel workings have attracted many birds, among them herons and a sizeable 'seemingly resident' flock of Canada geese.

And what of that other water? The river Severn is only a few yards away. Thankfully, the village is up the hill and out of floods' way, though there are some river meadows that are occasionally underwater. There are the Holt Locks, the weir and some excellent fishing, with a few salmon caught most seasons.

Hopwood 🌿

Hopwood, a hamlet within the parish of Alvechurch, lies at the northern end of the county. Hop is a Saxon name for hill, so Hopwood means hilly-wood; the hill remains, but not much forest, although the National Trust owns Hopwood Dingle, a beauty spot on the hamlet's north-eastern boundary. It is a long, straggling village, a ribbon development along the A441 on its way towards Redditch and the Vale of Evesham.

Hopwood has a picturesque village hall. Previously the building had belonged to the adjoining Southan's Hopwood Brewery, who had used it for the manufacture of mineral waters. The brewery was noted for its pure spring water. After being demolished the site was used for a club, and is now a motel.

Across the road stood Hopwood Church, an outpost of Alvechurch Church, which was demolished because of insufficient support. Further down the hill the road crosses the Worcester-Birmingham canal. This was once the nucleus of the hamlet.

The Post Office and Stores, opposite the present Hopwood House Hotel, had once been a canal-side Inn where 'leggers' called to eat, drink and rest and dry their clothes after legging their narrow boats through nearby one and a half mile long Wasthill Tunnel. The sound of a noisy tug which was used to tow narrow boats through the tunnel was a familiar sound to many residents.

Further along the road a lane on the left leads to farms and two Birmingham Sports Clubs. The latter moved here because they found some (rare) level ground. The new approach road to the recently opened

M42 is a little further on, alas Hopwood's peace and quiet are no more. Land has been cut-up, lanes severed or destroyed. One of the oldest and most beautiful farms, tended by generations of the Bushell family, has been lost. Pestilence Lane has vanished, it was so called because victims of the Black Death are reputed to have been buried there. (Nearby 'Jingle Joys Farm' was once called 'Black Pits Farm).

Continuing along the road one arrives at Arrowfield Top, one of the old Worcestershire field names. A sense of history still lingers on turning sharp left along the Old Birmingham Road where there are several old cottages and small holdings.

In 1875 the Birmingham Children's Hospital formed a 'Samaritan' fund; to provide after-care and convalescence for child patients. In 1879 they rented two cottages at Arrowfield Top, where children could spend a month or more recuperating. In those days Hopwood was very isolated and the Tangye family who had connections with the local Cadbury family provided a donkey, carriage and harness so that children could be transported from the nearest Railway Station to the cottages.

The donkey and carriage was very popular with the children who benefited from the fresh air rides around the countryside. In 1890 Richard Cadbury gave Moseley Hall for use as a children's convalescent home. Arrowfield Top consequently closed in 1891. In its last report the Hospital Committee expressed some regret for the closure of the little Home at Arrowfield Top where 1,383 children had been received with very few mishaps.

Ipsley

Ipsley, or Epeslei as it was named in the Domesday Book, was originally a Saxon clearing in the Forest of Feckenham. When the Normans came, the Saxon land was given to Norman soldiers as a reward and Ipsley became part of the vast estate of Osburn, who in turn 'let it' to Hugh Huband whose family lived at Ipsley for 700 years.

The settlement went into decline during the Middle Ages (the Black Death could have been the cause) and eventually only the church (built in the 13th century), the watermill, Ipsley Court and the Mill House were left. In the 1950s the watermill became very dangerous through vandalism and had to be demolished. The Court, so long ago damaged by fire, was rebuilt in the 1980s, and the church and Mill House are much as they ever were – one at the top of the hill, the other at the bottom.

Walter Savage Landor the poet, born 30th January 1775, lived at Ipsley Court for his early years, and mentions Ipsley Alders in one of his poems.

Now Ipsley is part of the New Town imposed on Redditch in the 1960s. New houses have been built and consequently the church has the largest parish in the whole county. Should all the parishioners attend the service at the church, even the whole of the church plus the churchyard would not be able to hold them all!

Trees are all around, because since the big tree planting year in 1973 (Plant a tree in '73) over 2,000,000 trees have been planted in and around Redditch, and this includes Ipsley.

Kemerton

'A long straggling agricultural village, charmingly situated on the south side of Bredon Hill', is how Kemerton has been described. Kemerton was mentioned in the Domesday Book and was in Gloucestershire until boundary changes in 1933.

The parish extends to the top of Bredon Hill and embraces the ancient camp. The Banbury Stone stands on the edge of the camp, known locally as the Elephant Stone. The custom is to climb the hill on Good Friday and kiss the stone. Tradition says that on a clear night when the bells of Pershore Abbey can be heard, the Elephant Stone clambers down the hill to drink from the river Avon.

At the highest point on Bredon Hill is a square tower known either as Parsons' Folly or the Summer House. This folly was built by Mr Parsons of Kemerton in the 18th century and can be seen for miles around.

The highest house in Kemerton is Bell's Castle. This was converted from two cottages into a castle with battlements by Edmund Bell, a sailor, in 1825. Many legends exist about his smuggling activities. They believed he preyed on French ships and had his loot smuggled up river to Bredon and taken up the hill by packhorse or secret tunnel.

Lower down is The Priory, with its beautiful gardens of rare plants, open to the public in summer. The houses in the village are varied and picturesque, with Cotswold stone, timber framed thatched cottages and red brick houses. The brooks running down from the hill are an attractive feature of the village as are the tidy gardens. There is a public house and a doctor's surgery. Years ago most villagers would have worked on the land but now most commute to other places of work, although there are quite a few craftsmen living in the village. Kemerton has a post office, a general store and a family butcher.

The parish church of St Nicholas was rebuilt in 1848 after much controversy in the Victorian Gothic style. Only the medieval tower remains of the original church, although a photograph hangs inside the church. Kemerton was the first in England to have surpliced choir. In the churchyard is a statue of an angel and it is said that if you should touch the middle finger of the outstretched hand you will have nightmares. She is also thought to walk at midnight.

The Roman Catholic church is dedicated to St Benet. It was consecrated in 1843. St Benet's has some of the finest old vestments in the country.

The village school, built in 1847 at a cost of £700 was closed in 1965 and converted into flats. The young children of the village now go to the neighbouring village of Overbury to school.

The village hall was completed in 1902 and named in memory of Queen Victoria. This is still a focal point for the villagers with many events and activities taking place there, catering for all ages, from baby clinic to senior residents.

During the Victorian era there were many large families – the Smiths, Morrises and the Figgots while Mr and Mrs Twilton had 25 children! The oldest family name is Dudfield, mentioned in 1585. Descendants of all these families still live in the village.

Kempsey ✤

Kempsey village straddles 3½ miles of the A38 four miles south of Worcester, bounded by the river Severn to the west and Kempsey and Stonehall Commons to the east.

It is one of the oldest, if not *the* oldest village in Worcestershire, taking its name from Kemeys, a Saxon chieftain in AD 799. Kemey's eye or Kemey's island was where the settlement lay between the river Severn and Hatfield Brook, and means a watery place, or place of sluggish (ie slow moving) water. There was a settlement here *before* that, dating back to the Iron Age.

Roman roads, 'Streets' or 'Ways' are in common evidence. Lyf's Lane, derived doubtless from the family of Lyf, was a 'Via Regia' and led to

King's Hill. The present 'Rocky Way', once called Angell Lane, led to the earlier Celtic fortification where during the campaign of AD 50 a chain of forts along the river was built to protect the conquered territory. The Camp which was in full view of the British Camp on the Malverns was supposed to have accommodated about 1600 men. The working of gravel pits within or near the site have swept away many features, but there is still part of the steep escarpment (west of Court House) near the river, built on top of the 'agger' or bank which surrounded the settlement and camp. Roman coins, tiles and the famous inscribed stone, one yard long and half a yard wide, was dug up in 1818 in the Vicarage kitchen garden. The sites of two villas, (Roman country estates) are still marked on the Ordnance maps. Many of the relics and finds can be seen in the Worcester Commandery and Foregate Street Museums.

The only association with the Normans is the mention in the Domesday survey when it was called Chemsege. In 799 there was a monastery at Kempsey and later a stone-built church. A country palace was built in the field west of the church, and Bishops of Worcester, with their retinues, were rowed down the river to entertain kings with their queens and courts. The Bishop's Palace finally fell into disuse and decay, was ruined by Tudor times and completely demolished leaving no trace.

Edward Winslow of Kerswell Green was one of the few Pilgrim Fathers who survived the Mayflower's voyage to the New World in 1620.

In 1649 Cromwell's troops were responsible for the battering down of the old church, and flattened the nose of every statue there lying. They also used a cottage, (still inhabited in Church Street) as a hospital for their wounded. Later it was the village laundry where washing was rubbed over the cobblestones in water from the nearby brook, and later still was the Cobbler's Cottage and it still bears that name.

In 1688 elm trees were planted in various parts of the village, to 'commemorate that glorious era'. Most were cut down in 1779 before attaining their full growth. A magnificent elm, known as the 'Revolution Elm' or the 'Arbour Elm', or colloquially 'The Albion', stood at the western end of Church Street. It was over 300 years old and considered unsafe when cut down in 1974. Probably the huge pollarded elms in the churchyard are as old.

Famous families lived here for generations. Parts of The Nash are pre-Elizabethan, and Draycott, Napleton, Kempsey Lodge and others are extremely old properties. Maharajahs in all their finery and jewels were entertained at The Nash at the time of Queen Victoria's Diamond Jubilee. Army generals, colonels and doctors retired here to live in the magnificent Victorian houses. Edward Elgar had two homes here, including Napleton Grange.

At a recent count there were over 40 organisations in the village from the baby clinic to play schools, an excellent primary school and clubs for young and old. Church and Chapel Fellowship Groups, Day Centre, County Library, Afternoon and Evening Women's Institutes, associations for young and old and for hobbies too. Gardening, photography, modern sequence and tea dancing, judo and a nationally known recording studio. There is something for everyone and Kempsey is a fantastic place in which to live.

Kington with Dormston 🎄

Snugly situated in the rural area half way between Worcester and Alcester, lies Kington village, which is separated from Dormston village by the A422, Worcester to Stratford road. The ancient black and white Red Hart Inn stands on the road as if on sentinel duty between the two villages. Both villages contain much that is of historical and architectural interest and importance.

St Nicholas, the 14th century church at Dormston, is one of the original 'forest churches', with a gabled half-timbered tower. Part of the old churchyard cross has been built into the church wall, and on the wall of the nave survive fragments of medieval wall paintings. The roof timbers have queen posts and the ancient font still has the staples which once secured the font cover. A young man from Dormston and his bride were married at the church in 1987. It was only the 103rd wedding to take place since registers began in 1843.

Dormston also boasts a Manor, formerly Bag End Farm, probably dating from around 1600. It is very picturesque, and has two dovecotes.

Nearby is Moat Farm House. The gabled house has the date 1663 carved upon its timbering. The timber frame dovecote here is a reminder of the days when fresh meat was virtually unobtainable in the winter and when doves were kept as much prized delicacies for the table.

St James' church, Kington with its particularly typical tower, is a fine example of the architecture of the year in which it was built. Inside, although the church was subject to some restoration work, parts of the 13th century nave and chancel survive, and the pulpit contains fragments of the medieval rood screen.

The Church of St James, Kington

Pottery, designed and produced by the local potter was made to commemorate the 700th anniversary of the church at Kington.

Unlike Dormston, Kington does not seem to have very many ancient buildings, apart from the Red Hart. Possibly the oldest farmhouse was demolished in the early 1960s. It was replaced with a modern version of the Manor House, complete with Lodge.

A farm building and one or two cottages show evidence of the old wattle and daub timber buildings and there are but two other examples of Victorian farmhouses.

Most of the buildings in Kington are of post-war construction. Fortunately such development has been restricted to 'filling in', turning what was once a small hamlet into a little village. One of the most interesting buildings which has been renovated is the Old Mill, situated on the stream near the main road. The owner has been farsighted enough to renovate the exterior and restore the Mill itself to working order. Mill cottages on the other side of the lane have been extended to form a residential home for elderly people.

On occasions Kington and Dormston have opened their villages to the public, to help raise funds for the two churches. At such times inhabitants were to be seen working long and hard, weeding, tidying the garden and mowing their lawns. Jeff the Potter, Beryl the Weaver, Eric the Painter and Tony the Taxidermist displayed their wares, along with the usual bric-a-brac offered on such occasions. Labouring for months in the background were ladies, sweating over hot stoves, turning out cakes and scones for the inevitable tea and cake stalls.

Knighton-on-Teme 🐿️

Knighton-on-Teme is a parish of some 450 people set pleasantly on the south-facing side of the Teme Valley, in the far west of Worcestershire. It is bounded almost entirely by streams and rivers. The most concentrated area of settlement is at Newnham Bridge, where houses of a variety of ages and styles are strung along the north side of the main road from Bewdley and Worcester as it snakes through the valley just above the flood plain. By contrast the remainder of the village is mostly an area of scattered houses and farms set on a plateau reached by lanes rising steeply from the valley.

Hops have been grown here since about 1600. The parish contains the northernmost hop-yard in the kingdom. Damsons are grown less and less but the blossom is still a feature in April.

Faintly visible are the hut platforms of the medieval village, probably deserted in 1348–9 when plague reduced the population of Worcestershire by 50%. The pattern of ridge and furrow of the old open fields can still be seen clearly at times.

The Norman church of St Michael stands at the centre of the medieval village, the only building to survive. It was built about 1120 on the site of an earlier one. The simple, cedar-shingled exterior of the belfry, popular with woodpeckers, hides one of the earliest and finest examples of timber-framing anywhere. It is supported by four massive cross-braced oak timbers. The church is also notable for important Norman detail wrought by the masons of the famous Hereford workshop. In the churchyard stands a medieval preaching cross remarkable for the niche in its western face.

The valley of the Teme funnels the main roads from Bewdley and Worcester, which unite at the river Rea bridge, westwards towards the attractions of Tenbury Wells and Aberystwyth, much used by summer holiday traffic. Parallel to it runs the course of the former Wooferton – Bewdley railway line, closed in 1962. The railway station at Newnham Bridge was one of the busiest on the line, seeing the despatch of large amounts of hops and fruit as well as passengers. After a period of dereliction it is now a shop and garden centre, complete with railway memorabilia.

Before the train the Knighton – Stourport canal was used, though it never reached Stourport. Coal was carried along it from the mines at Mamble to Tenbury. The enterprising can make the impressive walk across the substantial remains of the aqueduct over the river Rea, said to have contained three million bricks. Some of the canal's course is accessible by public footpaths from which the remains of locks and a wharf may be seen. In financial trouble, the canal was eventually bought by the Great Western Railway Company which built over part of its course.

The old school with its distinctive Boyles Ventilator visible in its airy position from many parts of the parish first opened its doors in 1875. In 1910, when the number of pupils had reached 120, it was extended but finally closed in 1983 when the number on roll had fallen to 15. The school's centenary was marked by appropriate celebrations and entertainment by the children who appeared in Victorian dress. The school and schoolhouse are both now private residences.

The Elizabethan farmhouse, hop kiln and other farm buildings at Lower Aston Court have been reclaimed from dereliction and now house a thriving pottery.

Leigh, Leigh Sinton & Bransford

Leigh (pronounced Lye), Leigh Sinton and Bransford are three closely-knit villages in the valley of the river Teme, roughly four miles from its confluence with the river Severn below Powick and some six miles west from Worcester, lying three or four miles north of Malvern and the impressive Hills. They are jointly and affectionately referred to as 'Leigh 'n Bransford'.

The parish church, with its massive square tower and, inside, the fine Norman arcade, is dedicated to St Edburga, grand-daughter of Alfred the Great. Her bones are enshrined in Pershore Abbey. The church stands near the Teme where it is joined by Leigh brook, also alongside the manor house, Leigh Court. In the gardens of Leigh Court stands a dove-cote remarkable for its nesting holes, 1380 in all, accessible by the use of a revolving ladder.

The 900-year old church is full of beauty and majesty. Originally lit by candles, then 56 oil lamps, electricity was installed just before the Second World War by the Norbury family.

The manor, the property of the Abbots of Pershore and later of the Sovereign, was, in 1590 granted to Edmund Colles by Queen Elizabeth I. He died in 1606 and lies in the church. A leather skull cap, placed on the sculptured head, is no longer in existence.

The huge tithe barn, next to Leigh Court and the church, was erected by the Abbots of Pershore in the late 13th and early 14th centuries. It is currently being restored by English Heritage. It is the largest full cruck building left standing in the world, measuring 140 feet in length, 30 feet high and 36 feet wide, containing ten bays and two wagon porches. On completion of the restoration, English Heritage will take over the guardianship of this historic building.

The modern bridge over the Teme at Bransford still bears traces of the old bridge which was erected in 1338 by the locally born Wulstan de Bransford, who became Prior of Worcester in 1317. The bridge sustained some damage during the Civil Wars.

On the hill-side at Bransford stands the tiny Norman chapel with a quaint wooden bell turret and oddly shaped 14th century doorway. The candlelit chapel is still in use today. It was used by monks as an overnight shelter while travelling from Gloucester and Tewkesbury to Worcester.

Leigh Sinton is a working village, basically unchanged over the years. The old wheelwright and coach builders was run by the Banner family for many years until prior to the Second World War when the present Jones family took over and still run a thriving and busy industry.

The Camelot Forge is the original blacksmith's shop and is still a focal point of village life. Pound Cottage is the only reminder of the Pound and the Toll House at the Hereford end of the village no longer extracts a toll from road users!

In more recent years the village hall was erected as a Memorial to those lost in the two World Wars and is for the benefit of all three villages.

The appearance of the countryside has changed recently with the loss of hops which were grown so extensively in this region. Together with fruit growing, they were the main crop. Farming is now mainly arable as well as producing apples, cherries, etc.

This corner of Worcestershire is steeped in history; its people are friendly; it is in the most beautiful countryside and is well worth a visit.

The Lenches

The villages of Church Lench, Rous Lench, Atch Lench, Ab Lench and Sheriffs Lench nestling in beautiful wooded and farmed hills, are together known as 'The Lenches'.

One local lady remembers the area after the Second World War, when the Lenches was still a farming community. Nearly all the families were related in some way or another. The peace and tranquillity radiated and, like so many other things from the past, have been lost for ever. Of course, in those days, there were only about four people who owned a motor car in the village; this in itself contributed very much to the peace of the place.

A living was to be made. A few hens, a pig in the backyard, a well stocked garden or 'piece' (a small plot of land), plums to be picked in bushel boxes for the contractors, apples plucked for store, cider fruit picked up and put into sacks to be sent to Bulmers – nothing was wasted. It was a very busy bustling, enjoyable way of life. Haymaking and collecting the corn sheaves was one of the favourites, anyone could join in, the merriment was better than any day out, life seemed like a big holiday! Standards were different in those days. It did not matter that there were no flush toilets and that you had to get water up in a bucket from the well in order to boil a kettle on the oil stove for a cup of tea. She remembers declining the offer of a bath simply because she was the fourth in line to use the same water with just a kettle full to warm it up!

Beehive Cottage at Church Lench

The villages are steeped in history, far too little is written down. There is a local book written by Dr Chafy called *The History of Rous Lench*. This gives much interesting information. Both Rous Lench and Church Lench have excellent churches which boast of Norman and Saxon origins. A brief history can be obtained from each of the churches for a small fee. Church Lench has been in existence for over a thousand years and is mentioned in the Domesday Book. The villages at that time belonged to the great Abbey of Evesham.

There are now many new houses, nearly all the old ones have been renovated, and in many cases extended to unrecognisable proportions. It is still a friendly place in a beautiful part of Worcestershire.

Lindridge 🦢

Lindridge is referred to in the Domesday Book, although then it was known as Lyderige.

103

The hall in which villagers meet was given to the parish by the Miss Wallaces, of a well known farming family. Their Eardiston Farming Company was sold off in lots in 1956. The family home was also sold and now houses several families after being made into flats.

The church had a large vicarage which also had the ghost of a monk. He was seen by a previous vicar's children and was said to be a friendly one. There were also other sightings of him at Lindridge House but the poor fellow was exorcised. The vicarage was bought privately and renamed The Priory, and a new vicarage was built. The school is still going strong with an attendance of 34 pupils.

An ancient knife made of green stone was found in a bed of gravel. This is in a Worcester Museum.

There is an excellent bus service. This was started in 1922 by two brothers, Mr Arthur and Mr Fred Yarranton and the same family are still keeping up its tradition.

There are the remains of a tunnel and various other pieces of what was to have been the Leominster Canal, intended to have linked up with the Severn. It was started in the 1790s. Unfortunately this never materialised and was finally closed in June 1858.

In the past there have been acres of hops and fruit to be picked. In September hop picking was a general holiday for Black Country folk. The lanes would be filled with song and laughter but modern machinery has taken that away. There are still a few hops to be picked but the rest is mainly down to grain, cattle and sheep farming now.

As the older people have died the houses have been sold and modernised and now the occupiers mainly commute to work. Their occupations are so different from the original farm workers – there are doctors, office workers, factory workers and salesmen.

Lindridge can boast two centenarians, one a gentleman who died just before his 104th birthday having lived the whole of his life within five miles of his birthplace. He walked ten miles daily to his place of work. The other was a charming old lady from Broom Bank.

There was a big weir at Meadows Mill where men belonging to the farm caught eels in traps. These were eaten by the local residents.

Little Comberton

Approaching Little Comberton along the Elmley Castle Road one is greeted by two cheerful mallards who live on the small pond between the early Victorian rectory and the 12th century church of St Peter. Then turning left or continuing along the main road there are to be seen on all sides beautiful medieval homes; some with gabled wings, one with overhanging timber-framed gable, another with a large dovecote in the garden. Some are thatched, others with mellow red-green tiles. They once housed the bakery, the forge, the village shop and the post office which have alas now gone in the name of progress. Do not go too fast as Little Comberton is a very small village nestling at the foot of Bredon Hill, so well loved by poets such as John Masefield, A. E. Housman and Sir Arthur Quiller-Couch.

The orchards of white blossom which used to be the provider of pears and apples for perry and cider making and plums for jam, have now disappeared from around the village along with the fields of flax. Bad seasons and economic changes in farming methods mean that jam is now only made in the home with fruit from the garden.

During the Second World War jam was an essential part of the nation's diet and in the small golden village hall which once housed the school, people would come from nearby villages to join the ladies of Little Comberton in making jam. The ladies would be handed the ingredients measured out meticulously by a Government Inspector, then the pans on the gas rings would bubble away and much satisfaction was gained knowing the people living in the misery of bomb-torn cities would be able to enjoy the goodness of the Vale's fruit.

Little Comberton is now no longer an agricultural village engaged in the production of cheese, flax and fruit. A large number of the inhabitants commute far to work, and the village has expanded along the narrow lanes with new housing. However the friendly community life is just as strong as it was in the busy days of the last century.

The Littletons ❦

The Littletons consist of three villages, South Littleton, Middle Littleton and North Littleton.

A landmark of South Littleton, the largest of the villages, is the maximum security prison, Long Lartin, as the spotlights surrounding it can be seen for miles around at night. The prison houses some 400 prisoners with 200 prison officers.

Another feature of South Littleton is a very picturesque thatched post

The medieval tithe barn at Middle Littleton   EV

office. The thatcher has left his trade mark of three straw birds sitting on the roof which looks very quaint.

There are two churches in the Littletons, the oldest being St Michael's situated in South Littleton. There is a recorded dedication of the church in 1205 but there was a church here in the 12th century. Of interest on the eastern jamb of the main door-way is a small consecration cross and over the chancel door and window, carved dropstones to represent the heads of a layman, an abbot or bishop and a horse or donkey.

St Nicholas' church in Middle Littleton appears to date from the 13th century although no record of the date of dedication is known. The bell tower holds six bells which are rung regularly for evening service by local bell-ringers.

The 140 foot long tithe barn is a feature of Middle Littleton and dates from the 13th or 14th century. It was given to the National Trust in 1975 by the owner of the manor farm to whom it belonged. It was lovingly

106

restored to its present glory by the Pilgrim Trust, the Historic Buildings Council and the District and County Councils. Although it is used for agricultural purposes it is open to the public from 9am to sunset all the year round.

The village hall, built in 1937 is used by many organisations throughout the Littletons. In one of the small rooms at the back of the village hall is situated the Resource Centre which is equipped with office machinery by the Community Development Unit of Hereford and Worcester County Council. Here it is possible to print programmes, tickets, village magazines and the like.

Not all the activity of the village centres around the village hall however, as there is a very flourishing Green Bowls Club – both indoor and out, and a tennis club on South Littleton recreation field and football is played in the winter and cricket in the summer.

There are many lovely walks around the Littletons, including Windmill Hill which is owned by the conservation trust and is slowly being improved to make it easier for walkers, with more accessible stiles and footpaths. The Nature Reserve is a paradise for the lover of wild flowers and butterflies, with magnificent views across the Vale of Evesham. Most of North Littleton is a conservation area and it has many listed buildings.

Market gardening and farming are the two main forms of employment in the Littletons. Asparagus in season is one of the most popular Littleton crops and of course there is an abundance of plums. Roses under glass are also grown in South Littleton by Mr Thompson and his claim to fame is that he supplied some of the roses for the wedding of the Duke'and Duchess of York.

Little Witley 🌿

This tiny village in 1987 had just under 200 inhabitants – about the same number as in 1787. There have been people living here since before 1066.

Thankfully, the village has no street lighting, no pavements, and no shop; in fact it has virtually no amenities at all – which suits most of the people living there!

The present population is a mix of farming families and commuters. One group making its living on the land, the other group returning gratefully to its tranquillity each day.

It is a very active and close knit community, with a busy social life, based on its church, the WI and the restored village hall, which now boasts a confortable licenced bar. Both groups have integrated well and virtually everyone in the village knows each other.

Sitting in a sheltered valley between Woodbury Hill and the Abberley hills, most houses in Little Witley have a view of one or the other. Woodbury Hill has on its summit a camp, believed to have been used by Owyn Glyndwr, the Welsh chieftain, when he plundered Worcester in 1405, before being pursued back over the Welsh border by Henry IV.

Two miles to the west is the now ruined mansion of Witley Court – the magnificent home of the Earls of Dudley, still Lord of the Manor of the Witleys. Although ruined, it attracts many thousands of visitors each year.

A few minutes by car from the village will bring you into the lovely rolling landscapes of the Teme Valley – surely one of the most beautiful parts of England.

The surrounding land is still largely farmed, being a mixture of arable, pasture and woodland. Bulmers, the famous cider makers, have one of their major orchards on the outskirts of the village – a beautiful sight in the spring with over 200 acres of apple blossom.

With many public footpaths leading from the village, walking amid lovely and unspoilt countryside is easy for villagers and visitors alike.

There are few very old houses in the village, but there are several 16th and 17th century cottages and farmhouses – mostly now restored, one of which is reputed to be haunted! The little church of St Michael and All Angels was rebuilt on a very old Saxon foundation in 1867, in the Early English style.

Most of the modern houses in the village have been built in the last 20 years and many of the old barns have recently been converted into dwellings. Overall, the village is well kept and attractive, with a high standard of garden.

However, Little Witley *is* becoming very well known as a traditional jazz centre! The village hall has been visited by the famous Humphrey Littleton on several occasions and bands from Holland and Sweden have also appeared, always to packed houses!

In a busy and stressful world, Little Witley is still largely as it has always been – tranquil, relaxed, informal and friendly – which is what village life is all about. Long may it stay that way.

Longdon

Longdon lies in the south of Worcestershire, bordering on Gloucestershire. Its boundaries are extensive. The village originally consisted of the church, vicarage, Churchend Farm, Manor Farm and the Moat House. There was a public house, the Plough, and a beer house called The Farmer's Arms. There were also several farm cottages, one of which became the post office. On the roads leading out of the village there are Chambers Court, Hillworth Court, Parsonage Farm and Wheypools Farm, and two old black and white half-timbered houses, Eastington Hall and Longdon Hall. There are several old half-timbered cottages on all the roads leading out of the village.

In the 1930s four council houses were built and in 1947 and 1954 two estates were built. In 1930 a village hall was erected in the middle of fields. It is now surrounded by houses. There has also been some private building, but only as infill.

The first recorded mention of a church at Longdon appears in a Charter of King Edgar to Pershore Abbey in AD 972. In the 14th century it was appropriated to Westminster Abbey. The tower dates from 1300, the nave 1785, the spire 1825 and the chancel 1870. The church and churchyard are very well kept these days but it was not always so. It is recorded that there came a time when someone dared to cut away a part of the precipitous churchyard, and a large portion was converted into a coach drive for the neighbouring house, now Manor Farm. Coffins with bodies in them were left 'standing out into the open day', and not until an order was obtained from the magistrates in Upton, was the present wall built at the east end of the churchyard, to hide the shameful work.

There has been a school and schoolmaster in Longdon since 1629. In 1846 the school was in ruins and a new school and house were built where they are now – on the site of the poorhouse. In 1833 40 children were taught reading, writing and arithmetic. The number in 1867 had risen to 90, each paying 1d – 2d a week. At present there are 34 children in school.

Longdon Marsh lies to the west of the village. It is said to be the remains of the great tidal estuary of the Severn. It still floods when there is a lot of rain in Wales.

During the Second World War there was a bombing range on Longdon Marsh and the flares were dropped on cotton parachutes to provide light for the dropping of smoke bombs. Many a parishioner wore underwear made from cotton parachutes!

Low Habberley 🌿

Habberley was mentioned in the Doomsday Book as a 'berewick' of Kidderminster. The original manor house, which once stood on the site of Low Habberley Farm, was burned down in 1718. It had been occupied by the Crane family since before 1563.

Habberley Valley is a well known beauty spot where the families of Kidderminster weavers and Black Country workers have for many generations mingled together for weekend and holiday respite away from their industrial pattern of homelife.

The valley is a survival from the days before mankind's arrival when England was divided from Wales by the Severn Straits, an arm-of-sea running from what is now the Bristol Channel to the Cheshire coast. In this area of Worcestershire the coast of the Severn Straits was indented by bays, hollowed by waves out of the side of the hills: Habberley Valley is such a bay. Much later, when the waters receded it became a backwater, then a salt marsh. Even today species of flora and fauna can be found in the valley which normally grow near the coast and flocks of seagulls return each year as though memories of the secluded bay have been passed down through the species.

A prominent feature of the valley is the dominant Peckett Rock, a survival of red sandstone eroded by the waters of the Straits, rising vertically with gullies up to 20 inches deep, worn through the years by the tread of human feet.

Members of the Waldron family lived and farmed at Low Habberley for 150 years, renting the farm from the Crane Estate, which included the golf course land, High Habberley and Habberley Valley. An amusing feature of the farm was the privy, a two-holer with a three-holer backing onto it, surely a necessity when 14 children at once were brought up there!

Just before the turn of the century a Mr Harvey Jennings who dwelt in one of the cottages in Low Habberley set up roundabouts and swings in the bowl of the valley floor. His son, Frank, born in 1900 continued the business, first living in a caravan and then moving into a small cottage. He and his wife began an ice-cream business by making it in a large pan over an open fire.

The Jennings' along with other local families, catered for charabanc parties from the Black Country, providing breakfasts and teas for many hundreds of people who came to spend their weekends and holidays under canvas amidst the scenic beauty and abundant fresh air of Habberley Valley.

Lower Moor ෴

Lower Moor is a village with 500–600 residents, between Wyre Piddle and Fladbury. There is a shop with post office, a Country Club, a village hall and recreation ground, and a small Victorian church which is part of the parish of Fladbury, Moor and Wyre Piddle. There are a number of black and white and thatched cottages, and the remains of a cider press have been preserved.

Farming and market gardening provided the main employment for villagers in the past. Although some are still employed on the land, there is now a good mixture of people, some work in nearby towns, others commute farther afield, and some are retired. Men who worked on the land would often wear cord trousers tied at the bottom and at the knee, and a shirt with a red and white kerchief at the neck. A plaited straw pouch on their backs contained their food and drink.

The village has never been wealthy and in times past some residents were really poor, with children having to wear outworn shoes and clothes. Many families kept pigs and hens and grew their own food, so they were reasonably well fed.

There was no public house, but there were two shops, one with the post office and the other had an off-licence. Faggots were made at the post office and sold for 1½d each, collected in basins brought by the customers. The 'travellers' who came to the area for pea and plum picking would have letters written for them at the post office. The first telephone was there, as was the public library. Gas came to the village in 1934 so homes had gaslights, but there were no street lights. Mains electricity did not arrive until 1947. The first Parish Council was formed in 1894.

The recreation ground in the centre of the village used to be hedged and was grazed by sheep. Now it has been opened up and is neatly mowed. There used to be a very tall elm tree near the playing field, called the Arbour Tree, which provided shelter from sudden showers. Nearby was a wall which children used for ball games. For many years the girls of the village took a portable maypole decorated with ribbons and hemlock around the village to raise funds for Pershore Cottage Hospital. The older girls taught the younger ones and they wove the ribbons as they

111

danced, singing two verses with the refrain, 'All around the maypole, trip, trip, trot, see what a maypole we have got, ribbons at the bottom, bosses at the top, all around the maypole, trip, trip, trot.'

Upper Moor is a hamlet of 17 houses. It lies between Wyre Piddle and Lower Moor. Hill is a hamlet of 12 homes, situated on rising land to the north of Lower Moor, looking across the plain of the river Avon towards the north side of Bredon Hill. Two of the houses bear the dates 1615 and 1713.

Hill Furze is a hamlet of about 16 houses and has a bird farm which is open to the public. On Good Friday Sunday School children used to go to Badger's Wood to collect primroses and violets.

Madresfield ﹏

Madresfield is so small a community that it almost fails to qualify as a village, but it has a 'big house', a post office and shop, a church, a school and a men's club. It also has one of the oldest WIs in Worcestershire, founded in 1917.

Madresfield Court, which has been owned by the same family since around 1160, is the main focus of attention for visitors, although not open to the public. But they are admitted to the grounds and maze occasionally, in aid of various charities, and always for the Agricultural Show on the Late Summer Bank Holiday. This show, which attracts about 12,000 visitors, is one of the very few of its kind in England still privately organised.

In the grounds you can see rocks that look natural, but are man-made; a grave that holds no man; a monument that bears no name; and the site of a church that had no foundations!

The rocks were made from the ruins of an old mill which collapsed 125 years ago. The grave, marked by a headstone with a Latin epitaph, is that of a famous horse, *Shadrach*, who carried Lord Raglan at the Charge of the Light Brigade, but was later killed in a hunting accident. In contrast, the most distinguished of the Earls Beauchamp, the 6th, is commemorated by a Celtic cross near the house, which shows only the date of his death – 19th February 1891 – for he had forbidden the erection of any memorial bearing his name, and he is buried in an unmarked grave in the church-yard. Behind this cross is a small railed area, site of an Anglo-Saxon church taken down in 1852 and replaced by a church whose foundations were omitted after the architect became insane. Twelve years later the building was declared unsafe, and the present church erected on a new site.

When the grounds are open for charity, you may have tea in The Playroom, a large room in the stables block. It gained its unusual name as venue for several theatrical productions staged there by the young family at the Court early this century, and later by the local amateur dramatic society. Now its role is often that of a village hall.

Sadly, Madresfield's only historic landmark, apart from the Court, was destroyed by the County Council in 1979. The Waterloo Oak, planted on the road to Newland by General Henry Lygon, later 4th Earl Beauchamp, who served under Wellington, was felled almost without warning, at the time of the last Earl's death. Lady Beauchamp planted a replacement in his memory. It is also a symbol of hope that new life may combine with old traditions in a

> 'village where Old Time stands still,
> gazing at the ageless Hills'.

Malvern Wells & The Wyche

Malvern Wells and The Wyche is situated on the eastern side of the 9 mile long Malvern Hills which form a part of the boundary between Worcestershire and Herefordshire.

Malvern Wells and The Wyche (or South Malvern) are two of the 'Seven Sisters'. The others consist of West Malvern, North Malvern, Malvern Link, Great Malvern and Little Malvern. They are strung along the roads which encircle the Malvern Hills, this area being one of outstanding natural beauty.

Above Malvern Wells and the Wyche rise Pinnacle Hill and Perseverance Hill. It is ideal walking country with criss-cross footpaths which provide gentle as well as strenuous climbs, rewarding walkers with magnificent views and a wealth of nature's colours. Buildings climb dizzily up the sides of the Hills, and trains run through them in a tunnel from the Wyche on the east side to Colwall on the west side.

On the Wells Common and on the Hills, sheep graze, wandering at will, crossing roads at their leisure – motorists beware, the sheep have right of way!

The Holy Well is situated on the hill high above St Peter's church. The well water is believed to have healing properties when used with faith.

In Victorian times people flocked to Malvern to take the 'water cure' and enjoy its fashionable Spa, staying at local hotels and lodging houses. One hotel, which had a popular pub, is now a block of flats, another is a school and a third is still a family hotel.

There were select girls schools, now converted into flats or 'Bed & Breakfasts'. The oldest building is a well-kept 18th century house called The Ruby after Admiral Benbow's last ship. A private residence retains the name The Old Bake House.

The architecture of dwellings is Victorian, Georgian and modern. In the times of Edward I and later, kings hunted in the forests which then existed. Now hang-gliding and golf are some of the sports indulged in.

Sir Edward Elgar, the great English composer, lived in Malvern Wells at one time and often walked on the Hills. His grave is in nearby St Wulstan's churchyard.

Before the Second World War the village was self-contained, enjoying its own grocery, butcher, doctor's surgery, chemist, fishmonger and post office. These amenities have disappeared and now there are only three general stores (one of which incorporates a post office) and two hairdressers.

The Village Institute hall is put to good use – mostly by the very young, the housewives and pensioners. The young adults, most of whom own cars, go further afield to work and for entertainment.

Mention should also be made of Little Malvern Priory which dates from 1125 when it was a monastery. The only part of the monastic buildings to survive the Dissolution was the part now known as the Prior's Hall which forms part of Little Malvern Court. The Court still belongs to the Berington family, descendants of John Russell who leased the Priory and its lands after the Dissolution. Only bare fragments of the original church remain today, Bishop Alcock was responsible for the initial restoration and many things have been done over the centuries. Recently much beautification of the interior has been done by the Society of Friends of Little Malvern Priory.

Mamble, Bayton & Clows Top

Mamble has a very old church with a Roman Catholic chapel built on the side, a very unusual occurrence. It is the village mentioned in the poem by Drinkwater. There is a local story which tells of a bloodstain on the stairs of the village pub, where a duel was fought, which can never be cleaned off.

114

Bayton lies on a loop off the main road. It also has a beautiful church overlooking the Clee Hills, which has a Norman doorway. Shakenhurst, the hall, means sanctuary, as it was in olden days. Legend has it that the Catholic Mawley Hall and the Protestant Shakenhurst were always quarrelling and the witch of Mawley put a curse on Shakenhurst, saying that never would a son inherit the estate. It has always passed through the female line.

Clows Top has grown up around a few cottages and is now as big as the other villages.

Martley

Mertelai, 'the wood of the martens'. Does the wood exist today or has that gone with the martens (a kind of weasel) and the original church? Domesday doesn't say more about the village except that there was a mill and 2 weirs, producing 2,500 eels and 5 'stitches' of eels. Nor does it mention St Paul's Well, sited below the church and thought to have been used for baptisms before the church was built.

The church dates from the 12th century and is mainly red sandstone, probably quarried from the Scar in the village. The oak beams and medieval wall paintings were exposed during restoration work in 1909, after an appeal raised over £2,000. A 15th century alabaster figure of Sir Hugh Mortimer and an even older marble or alabaster tomb occupy oppposite sides of the chancel. The oldest complete set of 6 bells in England were cast at Martley in 1673 and refurbished and returned in 1983.

A school was started in 1315, classes being conducted by the chantry priest but it was later held in a succession of buildings, becoming a grammar school in 1577. There is still an infants and junior school for the village and a High School serving the surrounding area.

There are some lovely 16th and 17th century houses, including Jewry or Jury House, The Noak and Firs Farmhouse. The former rectory, now a private house, is cruck framed with some wattle and daub and has an Elizabethan staircase. Pudford Farmhouse is built on the former site of a convent, dating from about 1290 when the property was given to the nuns, of Westwood, Droitwich.

Very little new private building was allowed by the District Council until the old 19th century workhouse, the Red House, was demolished in the 1970s and a new housing estate built on the site.

Jewry House, Martley

Six smithies, all long gone, served the local inhabitants. Now the Central Garage services the vehicles of the present villagers and the Rogers family coach firm also provides transport. Many families have farmed the area for generations and several of the old field names still exist – Poppies Parlour, The Shells, Hopelands, Northlands. The red sandstone soil of the valley and the limestone around the hills enable all types of farming to be followed and much fruit is grown in the area, with commercial cider orchards and hop fields.

Many old trades have gone but two shops, a haulage contractor, a sawmill producing sheds and fencing, and various businesses on the trading estate provide employment today. Medical needs are met by a local surgery, manned by three doctors.

Buildings and history do not make a living community without a balance between work, play and entertainment. The village Memorial Hall plays host to archery, rifle shooting, keep fit, WI and the youth club and brings together the happy mix of families who live in Martley today. Some of these are discovering the village as a commuting base whilst others have many generations of ancestors buried in the churchyard.

Naunton Beauchamp 🐿

In AD 972 the village was known as Nauwenton and was a Saxon settlement of about 25 families, comprising a manor, a pound or market-place, a shrine and a watermill, all the essentials then for daily living. Even now, earthmounds provide evidence of longhouses which accommodated families and their animals, and the area round the likely site of the mill shows the irrigation system, which would have been essential for a comparatively large population.

With such a well established settlement, it may be wondered why it was ever abandoned, was it fire or floods or even marauders that caused a village to vanish? Yet, another village developed just a few hundred yards on the other side of the brook. No one knows the answer.

The present village is set in pastoral surroundings on Lias Clay, well watered by the Wixena Brook and the charmingly named Piddle Brook and as the area is only 90 feet above sea level, there is often some spectacular flooding.

On the approach to the village from the B4082 road is Naunton Court, a large black and white and stone-built house which stands beside the Saxon village area and, at the eastern edge of the present village, there is Naunton House. Centrally there are two other farms, Poplars and Claremont. All four are working farms. Also in the village are several large black and white houses, two of them thatched, and numerous country cottages, some having been carefully adapted to modern living and all of them contributing charm and interest to the village scene. The church of St Bartholomew, the rectory, a small village green and about 20 modern houses complete Naunton Beauchamp.

The population is about 100 and very few houses change ownership, thus suggesting that people come here to stay. Yet there is no shop, post office or inn, no school, no village hall, and the last bus left 15 years ago and has not been seen since. Postal deliveries are once daily at widely differing times but the postman will accept letters from householders.

117

Bread comes on three days a week, milk on four days and the library van once a month.

So, with such an isolated village, a close bond of friendship and neighbourly help is quickly to hand when the necessity arises but, even so, visitors sometimes ask whatever people actually DO? Horse riding is on the increase and several fields, once used for farming purposes, are now pony paddocks. Dog walking is a regular source of social activity and so is gardening with some residents keeping grass verges cut and maintaining the village green.

Naunton Beauchamp has an active Parish Council and a Parochial Church Council, also the Beauchamp Players, a drama group which entertains at the annual New Year party and produces plays for various festivals and drama competitions.

Norton Juxta Kempsey

Norton Juxta Kempsey lies four miles south-east of the city of Worcester and within easy access of the M5 motorway and Wales.

The old Anglo-Saxon name was Norotun, meaning North Farm or Homestead. But north of where? Possibly Kempsey, since the two villages were connected through the church. In the 14th century Juxta Kempsey was added to the name to distinguish it from other Nortons in the county.

The parish also embraces the hamlets of Hatfield, known in the 12th century as Hathfeld, meaning heather-covered open land, and Littleworth, meaning a small enclosure of arable land.

Since the latter part of the 19th century, Norton has perhaps been better known as the home of the Worcestershire Regiment. The Barracks were built in 1876 and the population census for 1881 showed 830 people living in the parish, 283 of them in the Barracks. Thus, Norton became a garrison village and St James the Great a garrison church, which accounts for the flagpole being in the churchyard instead of on the church tower, and for the Colours in the military chapel.

The present church, restored and enlarged in 1874, dates from Norman times, but it is possible a church existed on the site earlier than this.

In 1970 the Worcestershire Regiment amalgamated with the Sherwood Foresters and since then the Barracks have stood empty. A preservation order has recently been placed on the Keep. Some of the adjoining land is now used by the Worcester Norton Sports Club.

The village street, Wood Norton, near Evesham as it looked about 1900

The school was started in 1857 by the then 'perpetual curate' of the church, Henry Faulkner. Today it is housed in a very pleasant modern building in Littleworth. Littleworth also has the Methodist church which was built in 1881 on the site of a former chapel erected in 1835. Next to the Methodist church is an old cottage, once the home of Bruce Bairnsfather, the First World War cartoonist and creator of 'Old Bill'.

Around 1920, Mr Deakin, the owner of Norton Hall, built a jam and canning factory to deal with the vast amount of fruit grown on his own land and the surrounding district. Today it is the world's largest manufacturer of foundry crucibles.

Hatfield lies about a mile south of Norton and is a cluster of farms and old and new houses. One old house claims to have a friendly ghost who walks along the hall but never enters a room! Another old house is said to have been at one time an Inn and Post House. This, together with an old milestone in Hatfield, suggests that the lane was once an important road to, perhaps, Pirton Court.

Today many residents in the parish are professional and business people, commuting to Worcester and Birmingham, but there is still a good farming community.

In 1977 a new parish hall was built in Littleworth to replace an old hut in Norton. It is a well equipped and much used building with sports facilities, playing fields, tennis courts and children's play area. The Hall Management Committee organise concerts and social events during the year, ending with a Christmas Pantomime.

In addition to these activities, there are many thriving clubs and societies.

The parish is proud to have won the Heart of England Best Kept Village Trophy twice, in 1985 and 1987.

Oddingley

Today the peaceful green fields surrounding the little church of Oddingley present a picture of tranquillity oddly at variance with the dreadful crime committed there last century.

On Midsummer Day, 1806, whilst walking in those same fields, Oddingley's rector, Rev George Parker, was first shot and then bludgeoned to death in broad daylight.

The rector was a pleasant man, well-known for his generosity to the poor but perhaps a little too astute in business affairs for the liking of some of his parishioners. At any rate a fierce quarrel over tithes had broken out between Rev Parker and some local farmers led by Captain Evans from nearby Church Farm, a well-known magistrate in the area.

The angry old captain was heard to declare furiously that Parson Parker was a very bad man and that 'there is no more harm in shooting him than a mad dog'.

It was not Captain Evans, however, who murdered the rector but a Droitwich carpenter, Richard Hemming who, immediately after the shot was seen running away across the fields towards Trench Woods. He was seen both to enter and to emerge from the woods after which he completely disappeared.

It was 24 years before Hemming's fate was known. In January 1830, during the demolition of a barn at Netherwood Farm, Oddingley, a shallow grave was found containing a skeleton with a fractured skull. Hemming's wife, who had since remarried, identified him by his clothes and a carpenter's rule found with the body. A further inquest was opened at the Talbot Inn in The Tything, Worcester.

The story was again told of the dispute between the unfortunate rector and Captain Evans and his friends. The inquest was adjourned and the

120

former occupant of Netherwood Farm, Thomas Crewes was taken into custody and held on suspicion of Hemming's murder.

Crewes made a statement disclaiming all responsibility for the murder but implicating Captain Evans and a man named Taylor who were both now dead.

The trial created enormous interest throughout the county. Crowds jostled for admission to the Guildhall where the case was being heard by Mr. Justice Littledale. After 13 hours the jury returned a verdict that Crewes was guilty as accessory after the fact. As he had not been charged with that offence the judge declined to accept the verdict. The jury then found Crewes not guilty.

When the news of the acquittal reached Oddingley the church bells were rung in celebration – much to the displeasure of the rector!

Offenham ✍🏻

Mention the name of Offenham and the first things that spring to mind are market gardening, glasshouses and the Maypole.

Market gardening was pioneered by James Myatt who raised in Offenham many new varieties of fruit and vegetables. His name and that of Offenham can still be found in seed catalogues. His vast influence on the village was commemorated by naming a housing development built in 1973 after him.

The Maypole, a village sentinel, has stood overlooking local events for many generations. There is no record of when the first Maypole was erected but they are known to have existed in medieval times, and it would seem that this is one of the few still in existence in England.

Offenham's wide Main Street is a mixture of black and white thatched buildings, cheek by jowl with more recent additions. A row of cottages, seven in all, have the distinction of being under one continuous thatch. These cottages, called Long Thatch, date from around 1463. Across the road Greywalls was the first school, later succeeded by the small parochial school in Ferry Lane, a Church school in 1873 and now a new school in 1987. The Malt House was the village shop for many years. Across its yard lay the dairy, bakehouse, malthouse and brewhouse with its fine copper boiler. Before the village hall came into existence this copper boiled the water for all communal events.

There is definite air of tranquillity to Offenham. No continuous drone of through traffic busy to be somewhere else. The Main Street branches at the Maypole and travels on to farm and field. Its unique position is the key to Offenham's more ancient past. Sheltered, fertile and in the bend of the river it encouraged Roman settlement. When it was made a gift to the Abbots of Evesham Abbey it soon became well loved. They built their Grange and deer park along with dovecotes. The present Court Farm and the Old Manor House are now all that remain. With the Dissolution, Evesham Abbey was demolished and almost all of Offenham Estate passed to Sir Philip Hoby and later to the Hazelwood family.

The church guards the entrance to the old village. Its origins date from Saxon times, of wooden construction it was rebuilt of stone after the Norman Conquest. Rebuilt again in 1450 it was served by the priests of Evesham Abbey. With the Dissolution came disrepair which led to rebuilding in 1861. Only the tower and the font are prior to this date. It is wonderful to think that Offenham villagers have brought their babies to be baptised in the same font for 500 years. The Cresswell family who have been master thatchers in this village for generations still pass the knowledge from father to son.

Buildings, methods of cultivation and life-styles change as an inevitable part of modern life. Nevertheless the fundamental things remain the same, the river, the fertile land and the heart of the village – its inhabitants.

Ombersley

Ombersley is a parish with ancient Saxon roots deeply embedded in fertile soil. It first appears in recorded history in the year AD 706 when it was given by a Deed of Gift to the Abbey of Evesham by Ethelweard. In the Domesday Book of 1086 it appears as Ambreslege, noted for its two cornmills and 15 hides of cultivated land. The word 'lege' meant a patch of ground that was a clearing in woodland, suitable for cultivation or a military camp.

The parish extends from Crossway Green in the north to Hawford in the south, and from east to west from the river Salwarpe to the Severn. Its soil is really an extension of the Vale of Evesham and hence farming and market gardening form the basic occupation of the area. This is reflected in the quality of exhibits on display each August at Ombersley Show.

Modern farming methods have led to the vacation of buildings now converted for residents who commute to neighbouring towns or who have retired. The present population is approximately 2,000. Many families still live here today whose forbears have been living in Ombersley for centuries.

The once heavily wooded valley has given a rich heritage of half-timbered houses. The greatest concentration of Listed Buildings built between 1450 and 1750 lies within a few hundred yards of the roundabout at the centre of the village. Twenty-eight houses are so listed. Of the present fine mature trees around the village the limbs of a huge old chestnut beside the roundabout stretch right across the road. The unusual fiery red of its autumn leaves is a breath-taking sight.

St Andrew's church with its splendid spire is an excellent example of the work of Thomas Rickman. It was built in 1829 to replace the much older one built in 1269 which had become unstable. The Old Chancel which is a fragment of this, remains as the private chapel of the Sandys family. The present church has a fine team of bellringers, a good choir, and a talented group of flower arrangers.

The Manor of Ombersley came into the possession of the Sandys family in 1560 when Edwin Sandys was appointed Bishop of Worcester by Queen Elizabeth I. Ombersley Court was built for the first Lord Sandys in 1724. Among the many fine trees surrounding the house is a huge Wellingtonia planted by the Duke of Wellington about 1849 and now over 118 feet in height. A Queen Anne house in the village bears his name, and a surgeon from his victorious army at Waterloo occupied the house in retirement.

Included in the many interesting half-timbered houses are Thatched Cottage on the main road, Cresswells, a distinguished cruck house at the roundabout, and the Dower House some yards further on. This was an old Court House where the Abbots of Evesham used to transact the business of the Manor Court until the Dissolution in 1539. The Kings Arms, originally built about 1450, has an early 17th century plaster ceiling and a solid walnut bedstead, said to have been slept in by Charles II after the Battle of Worcester. Whether that tall monarch had a comfortable night is not recorded: the bed is remarkably short. Another pair of cottages nearby used to be the Pewterers' Guild House in Bewdley. It was bought by a redoubtable member of the Sandys family, the Dowager Marchioness of Downshire, for the sum of £32 and the timbers transported from Bewdley to its present site where it was re-erected in 1841. The former forge at Sinton is marked by a horse-shoe shaped door. The oldest bowling green in England is at Hadley, the original Bowling Green Inn being built during the reign of Elizabeth I.

Ombersley did not escape the ravages of the plague. On a little green in the centre of the village is a large stone trough. This Plague Stone was moved from the old pack-horse road, west of the Court. When in its original place, it warned travellers to keep away and formed a receptacle for food for the beleaguered villagers to collect.

The parish has two excellent endowed schools, two doctors with their own dispensary, a post office, and no less than six inns in Ombersley alone. The village is well off for shops. They include a baker who bakes his own bread, a butcher who kills his own meat, a grocer who specialises in cheeses and wines, and a craft shop.

Overbury ✒

Overbury is situated on the lower southern slopes of Bredon Hill, around a stream which has provided water for the houses and farms and power for the mills over many centuries. There were two Iron Age forts on the Hill, the Romans were here and it seems to have been inhabited ever since. The church is Norman in origin, there was an Elizabethan manor house, and parts of many of the houses dated from medieval times. The present village is part of the Overbury Estate, owned by the Holland-Martin family of Overbury Court. Almost all the houses in the village are owned by the estate, which farms the surrounding land as well. In the last century there was always plenty of work available on the estate, its farms, gardens and houses for all who lived here.

Before the First World War the village was cared for in a very real way by the Martin family. The school children were provided with clogs and cloaks, a good soup once a week in winter, and plenty of prizes to encourage excellence in class. For everyone there were plays, whist drives and dances in the village hall and 'Pleasant Sunday Afternoons' organised by Lady Martin when anyone could go to the village hall to hear a speaker or just have a chat.

Overbury Flower Show was a great annual event, and prizes given on that day included Best Kept Pigsty and Best Crop of Wheat.

Today much has changed, although there remains an estate which employs most of the villagers. The estate still employs a plumber, carpenter and gamekeeper, woodmen, gardeners and farm workers, but now has garage mechanics, secretaries, a computer operator and an accountant. Also in the village are a farrier and a glass engraver, security photographer, smocker, seamstress – all new small businesses. One shop remains with post office, the school and church are still here, but the policeman and vicar have gone and services must be shared with other villages. Under fives, Girl Guides and senior residents all meet outside the village and the cricket and bowls teams contain few actual residents of Overbury, but all these activities are thriving. Village activities such as the annual street market, bonfire night and occasional dances are well supported. The school has re-introduced the annual Maypole dancing ceremony, and there is still a team of church bell ringers. The fabric of the village is still well cared for by the estate and the whole place has a tidy appearance.

It is still very much a working village with plenty of young people as well as old. Some have come to the village from elsewhere to work for the estate, many are from old-established Overbury families with three generations in the village. People often stay on after retirement and sons and daughters still seek a job here and a house to go with it. As machines have replaced people in both domestic and farm work, so fewer people are employed and occasionally there is a cottage available for an 'outsider'. Thus the village has been able to break away from the feudal atmosphere and support a wide cross-section of the community without losing all the advantages of feudal patronage.

Pebworth 🌿

The parish of Pebworth lies in the north-eastern corner of Worcestershire, bordering on the counties of Gloucestershire and Warwickshire. From the time of Pebba, the Anglo-Saxon owner who gave the village its name, it has grown to the present community of over 600.

The focal point of the village is St Peter's church which dominates the ridge on which Pebworth is set. The 13th century church has many items of interest – a Jacobean pulpit, a 15th century font, boxed pews and a particularly bitter epitaph to the scalded child of a previous vicar. Recently villagers have raised enough money to restore a full peal of bells which now ring out over Pebworth.

Descending the hill from the wooded churchyard is Front Street where the village shop and post office is situated. Built of Cotswold stone and dating from the 18th century it is now the village's only shop. When snow lies on the ground Front Street becomes a paradise for children with their sledges.

Amongst many protected trees within the parish is the sycamore which stands in Back Lane outside the old forge. Here horses were tethered

Thatched cottages at Pebworth

whilst waiting to be shod. Further down Back Lane is the village school which was built at the turn of the century. The original bell still summons children whose grandparents were once pupils here.

Manor Farm adjoins the school field. This Georgian farmhouse was once the home of the Shekell family who owned most of the village in the 19th century and includes amongst its farm buildings a listed dovecote. The last member of this family to die in Pebworth was Rev Bonner Shekell who is buried in a spinney on the outskirts of the village. There are many tales explaining his final resting place – a long family feud, a dislike of the churchyard or did he just want a 'tomb with a view'?

Friday Street is reputed to have been the haunt of William Shakespeare and certainly many of the thatched and timbered cottages date from his time. Was it here that he is supposed to have written the rhyme about local villages?

> 'Piping Pebworth, Dancing Marston
> Haunted Hillborough, Hungry Grafton
> Dodging Exhall, Papist Wixford
> Beggarly Broom and Drunken Bidford'

The village extends eastwards from Friday Street to Broad Marston, a past winner of the Best Kept Hamlet award. Horticulture has always played a major part in the economy of Pebworth and nowhere is this more obvious than along Broad Marston Road where there remains evidence of market gardens. Today there are only a handful of families earning their living this way. As market gardens revert back to farmland it is good to see, however, that one of England's leading Pelargonium specialists has moved into redundant greenhouses and is benefiting the village through local employment and tourism.

At the centre of the village both geographically and socially are the local public house and the village hall. The Masons Arms provides a meeting place for villagers and supports teams for darts, dominoes and other traditional pub games.

Pebworth is fortunate to have a large village green known as the Close. Thirty years ago the Parish Council acquired this land from the Shekell estate, thus saving it from development and preserving it for the future. Today's children can now enjoy the delights of a playground built near the site of the old cider mill.

Pedmore

There are those who say that Pedmore is not a village, but only a dormitory suburb of Birmingham. Everyone goes elsewhere to their places of employment. However, there has been a village here since the Domesday Book mentioned 'Pevemore' at the foot of Wychbury Hill.

The church, dedicated to St Peter, has been rebuilt twice, once about 1250 and again in 1871. On the second occasion all was rebuilt except the tower, the south aisle and the porch. The north aisle was added, also the organ chamber and the rector's vestry. In the Rev A. E. Buchanan's time, 1913–1938, the choir included two members who walked 6 miles every Sunday. On Christmas Day and Easter Day these two members and others who lived locally attended the 8am Service and were entertained to breakfast afterwards in the Rectory.

Before the double track road swept away all before it, including a drinking trough for horses and the 'Lamp' there was a small public house called the Foley Arms on the main road. There is still a Foley Arms there today but it is a sophisticated Toby Inn with bright lights and is known for its grills. The 'Lamp' was a gas lamp put up in 1884 by Charles Evers Swindell at the crossroads. It was in a triangular garden surrounded by iron railings and must have been a great convenience to all passers-by.

The school in Pedmore was founded in the late 17th century and rebuilt in 1859/60 at the expense of the Feofees of Oldswinford Hospital. The earliest master was instructed to 'teach only English to the poor children', of whom there were 76. For 40 years from 1882 Mr Thomas Ager Greenfield was master.

Early organisations in the parish included the Girls Friendly Society, the Band of Hope and the Church of England Temperance Society. Ladies who were at the school around 1920 recall going on school trips by 'coach' to places like Habberley Valley – all of 6 miles away! Horse brakes used to make trips to Bromsgrove Fair and on May Day another village character, Mr Mills of Bank Farm, would dress up his horses with ribbons. Bank Farm has given way to a housing development; this contains Bank Farm Close to remind us of the past. Pedmore's population, which in 1881 was 500, is now 6,500.

Peopleton

Peopleton, originally Pyble's Den, meaning the farm of one Pyble, is a small village running alongside Bowbrook, some 3 miles north of Pershore. Until 1969, with a population of around 200, the village enjoyed a truly rural existence, with black and white listed buildings, several farms and a church full of historic interest, dating from the 13th century. In 1969 a small estate of modern houses was added, but this in no way detracts from the character of the village.

The village school, now a private dwelling, was closed after the Second World War, the increase in population to over 600 in 1969 being too late to reverse this decision. Apart from the church there is a small village shop-cum-post office, the Crown Inn and a somewhat inadequate village hall. On the outskirts of the village, land has been acquired in recent years for a children's playing field and cricket pitch.

By the playing field at the edge of the village, there is a village pump inscribed 'Erected October 1890 for the benefit of the cottages, Peopleton' and underneath is the information that it is a 'Frost protected lift pump'. This, presumably was the sole water supply for inhabitants other than those fortunate few who had wells on their own land. How we take for granted the turn of the tap!

One of the larger houses in the village, Bowbrook House, now an Independent School, was originally occupied by Caroline Baroness Norton, a benefactor of the parish, whose parish parties and Christmas gifts

Pinvin was an agricultural village with market gardening and fruit orchards. In 1928 a local grower pre-packed his produce for market. Most of the apple and plum orchards have been replaced by cereal crops and vegetables. A small trading estate on the edge of the village gives some local employment with a cement works, roadstone factory and a printing firm.

The main Hereford – London railway line runs through Pinvin, and Pershore station is within the parish. This once busy station now caters for a few stopping trains daily giving access to Worcester, Evesham and beyond.

Pinvin is a well watered place. Records show about 20 moats in earlier years. Two remain near the Manor House, village children still collecting tadpoles from them. Piddle Brook runs through the village to the river Avon, a local ditty being – 'Naunton Beauchamp, Peopleton and Crowle, North Piddle, Wyre Piddle, Piddle in the Hole'.

Spion Kop, named from a battle in the Boer War, is a small housing estate for retired people from surrounding villages. Nearby, a field gate has gateposts formed by gun barrels from the Boer War.

Many of the old characters of the village have vanished together with the roadsweeper and his barrow, the postman on his bicycle and the village policeman. One can only sum up the old villagers with this local saying –

'Us 'baint all green, if us be cabbage looking'.

Pirton 🌿

Pirton, situated 6 miles south-east of Worcester and spread round four lanes, is so small that newcomers frequently go through it without realizing they have arrived! It is first recorded in Saxon times, as 'Pyritune', meaning pear tree farm, and to this day many pear trees are scattered throughout the village.

The Norman church, from which there are fine views to Bredon Hill and the Malverns, stands at the eastern corner of the parish on the site of a Saxon building granted to Pershore Abbey in 972. This small church has a beautiful and unusual half-timbered, aisled tower which dates from the 14th century and replaces an even earlier central stone tower. In the chancel is a memorial, dated 1664, to Mrs Elizabeth Lole, whose husband, Rev William Lole, was rector from 1643–1671. Interestingly, direct descendants of theirs are now farming at Hermitage Farm about a mile from the church. Hermitage Farm has an unusual medieval dovecote and the house is thought to have been built on the site of the old manor of Pirton Power.

Formerly the village was entirely agricultural, but now only 2 or 3 farms remain, and most people work in the surrounding towns. A few of the old half-timbered and cruck-beam cottages are left, much restored, but many fell into complete decay this century and by 1951 it was a 'dying village of elderly people'.

However, after strenuous protests from the then rector and others, a number of council houses, old people's bungalows, and a small private development were built and the village is once again flourishing, though still small. At the time of the Domesday survey the population was 80, in 1851 it reached a peak of 240, and now seems settled at about 150.

Pirton had its own school from 1879 until 1952, and a general store already in existence in 1815, which survived until 1950. A small sub-post office managed to keep going until the early 1970s and in the last century there was a village blacksmith at the old forge. The coming of the Birmingham to Gloucester railway line in 1845 made the village less isolated as there was a halt and sidings on the eastern edge of the parish, and trains stopped until the 1950s, but now, like so many villages, Pirton is entirely dependent on private cars, as the last bus service vanished about 1972.

The ancient half-timbered Pirton Court at the southern edge of the village is, apart from the church, the most notable building. It stands on the site of a medieval moated manor, and in 1375 the then owner, William Folliott obtained a licence to celebrate service in his oratory at Pirton. It passed through various hands, and in 1663 came into the possession of the Coventry Family, who owned it until very recently. It was much added to in late Victorian times and became the home of Viscount Deerhurst, whose widow lived there until 1949. In the 1920/30s the visiting Test cricket teams were entertained at the Court when one of the Coventry family was president of the Worcestershire County Cricket Club, and to the delight of the villagers, they were able to watch (at a discreet distance!) the great Sir Donald Bradman play on the west lawn.

Poolbrook 🍂

Poolbrook is today one of the outlying districts of Malvern. While it has always been influenced by its large neighbour it still retains a sense of community.

The name is derived from the various pools which used to be situated in the area, including Bell's Pool, Aikley's Pool, Hunt's Pool and Hastings' Pool, and the brook which runs through the village off the Malvern Hills eventually joining the river Severn. Of these pools the only surviving one is Hastings' Pool. Many a motorist has come to grief against the railings around this pool on his way into Malvern from the east.

Poolbrook is now known for its common land. Bordering the main road is a wide area of common land maintained by the Malvern Hills Conservators – one of the oldest conservation bodies in the country. Not many animals graze on the commons these days, just the occasional tethered pony. It is only a few years since a flock of sheep grazed regularly, following the same route each day finishing up outside their owner's gate in Hayes Bank Road to be shut up for the night. Naturally the local residents enjoy walking across the commons with or without a dog, and horses and riders are often seen.

The village had two focal points for its activities; these were the church – St Andrew's church – and the Foley Institute. The church was not fully consecrated until fairly recently, being designated as a Chapel of Prayer.

The Foley Institute was built by Lady Emily Foley who was a local landowner and benefactress. It was used as a village hall and many activities were held there ranging from the monthly social meeting to a 'dame school'. Every month the villagers met for dances, singing and competitions. Whist drives were also held.

In former times most of the population were engaged in agriculture with cows and sheep to look after and crops of hay and wheat. Nowadays many are employed at the Royal Signals and Radar Establishment, in Great Malvern's shops, offices and schools or in Worcester.

The villagers were kept occupied by their labours and by the events of church and family life. Occasionally visiting entertainers gathered a crowd around them. One time a man came round with a dancing bear. The bear was brown and tied to a pole by a length of chain. A regular visitor was the hurdy-gurdy man.

The advent of war brought a new strong presence into Poolbrook. The research group 'Telecommunications Research Establishment' (TRE) came to the area and the workers were billeted on householders.

Later, new buildings were erected to house what became The Royal Radar Establishment and is now The Royal Signals and Radar Establishment. Many of Poolbrook's modern residents are employed there and most can see the familiar radar dishes from their windows as they look upwards to the wonderful Malvern Hills.

Pound Green & Button Oak

Pound Green and Button Oak are adjacent, on The Worcestershire/ Shropshire borders. Originally, Pound Green was part of the Arley Estate and Button Oak was in the Kinlet Estate. The whole area was covered by oak trees and known as the Wyre Forest. Local people lived in tiny cottages and worked for the estates. Gradually, forest land was cleared especially at Pound Green.

A claim of land could be made if a man and his helpers could make a clearing in the forest, erect a 'house' – chiefly a strong chimney – and have smoke going up the chimney within 24 hours; then he could have the land and settle there. On Pound Green Common, one unfortunate person did not get the 'smoke going up' in time so he lost his claim. The plot of land is still referred to as the 'Hovel' Orchard. This method of settlement might be the reason why many habitations are way off the beaten track. Several people on the Green still have the right to graze their animals on the Common and still do. The Pound, for straying animals and subsequent fine on collection, has now disappeared.

Button Oak is still remembered as a place of charcoal burners. It has been suggested that 'Button' is a corruption of 'Boothen' which is the old plural form of booth – a wigwam type of shelter where the charcoal burner lived while he controlled his charcoal mound, sometimes for five days.

Families also eked out a precarious living by the making of baskets and besoms and, of course, tree felling. The women often worked at bark stripping. The oak bark was used in the tannery at Bewdley. Their sheep, pigs and cows were allowed to wander in the Forest and often small bells were hung on a strap round the necks of such animals so they could be easily located by the sound. Every cottage had an orchard of damson, cherry, apple and pear trees. Cider making was a very important part of the family activities. When the Estates sold off part of the land, much of it was bought by Cadbury's and the Forestry Commission. Fences had then to be erected and the bells were no longer needed.

Plantations of conifers have replaced much of the oak but there is plenty of beech and existing oaks are left to mature. Dotted about are many old yew and holly trees. Bluebells and foxgloves abound but rarer plants are closely guarded. Fallow deer roam the woods and are, unfortunately, killed on the road by motorists. The adder population is studied by several local biologists and many people visit the Bird Sanctuary.

The village shop in Button Oak is built on the remains of an old Methodist chapel and at the side was the village school, now covered by a private dwelling. St Andrew's church opened in 1873 and Pound Green village hall was built in 1949. The local pub, also called the Button Oak, is an old building. Recently some wattle and daub was discovered during alterations. The old stone cottages, '2 up and 2 down', are now refurbished and extended as far as regulations will allow in a conservation area.

The Pound Green and Button Oak settlements do not have any famous historical sites but the Forest is still very much alive with people who appreciate what it has to offer.

Queenhill ❧

The hill that rises out of the valley of the Severn is called Queenhill. It does not take its name from any Royal Queen, but from the valley or 'cwm' over which it stands. No trace remains of the deserted medieval village, now ploughed out, or of the tithe barn which stood in the field opposite the church.

In 1074 the King held the Manor of Queenhill, his interest ceasing some two centuries later, which probably accounts for the fact that the Arms of England are depicted in 13th century glass in the church of St Nicholas, where Saxon and Norman features remain.

Beside the door, Henry Field, a member of a prominent Kings Norton family, stands in alabaster silence between his two wives, Anna and Sybilla. In 1554 Henry purchased the Manor of Holdfast and the tithes of Queenhill. In a lengthy will, dictated on his deathbed in 1584, he bequeathed 'To Eleanor Bough my procteridge tithes of Queenhyll during her lief (yf my wyfe think well of her behaviour) or else to be at my sayd wyfe's election to have the same herself'. Eleanor's behaviour evidently didn't come up to scratch, as the tithes passed to Sybilla!

Sir Edward Elgar, the composer, spent much time cycling around the area on 'Cabus'. It was while sitting in the porch at Queenhill church that he gained his inspiration for *The Apostles*.

The landscape lacks grandeur, but lush fields are grazed by cattle and sheep along the lane, which is a loop off the Longdon to Upton Road. To the east, the country undulates in gentle contours through which the river Severn meanders, Bredon Hill forming a backcloth to the tower of Ripple

Pull Court, Queenhill is now a boarding school

church; whilst to the south-west is the long range of the Malverns, where lights sparkle like diamonds in the darkening skies.

The lane, fingerposted one long mile from the main road, cuts downhill past the row of former council houses which perpetuates the name of Dowdeswell, a family who resided for centuries at Pull Court. It remained in Dowdeswell hands until 1934 when it became the home of Dick Seaman, one of the greatest racing drivers produced by England. He was tragically killed on the Nürburg Ring in Germany. It is now Bredon School, a boys boarding school.

There are some good houses in Queenhill and several pretty cottages up on Heath Hill. The picturesque Church End Farm is currently undergoing restoration and The Old House was modernised a few years ago. Cedar Bank was once the lodge to the great house. The black and white house, hiding behind a high Lleylandii hedge was originally the school founded by the Dowdeswells for the children of estate workers. It then became a Working Men's Club before its sale in 1932. Green Farm is an elegant Georgian house and Holdfast Cottage, situated on the Queenhill/Holdfast boundary, beside the old saltway, has recently undergone improvement. Sadly, Barley Cottage, is becoming derelict through neglect.

The manor house, which was 'Victorianised' by the Dowdeswells who also determined the present appearance of the church, was restored in 1973. Of 16th century appearance it has a medieval core and was once much larger. During the Civil War the owner, William Gowever, was called upon to house both men and horses and his account of all payments and losses sustained by the Parliamentary forces during the siege of Gloucester, makes interesting reading.

In the 14th century a windmill was held with the Manor. Today, in a ploughed field near the site, and unknown to many a passer-by, is a memorial inscribed, 'To the memory of Dick, the favourite horse of his kind master, RLF 1870'.

Ripple ◈

The village of Ripple lies on the southern edge of the county, bordering Gloucestershire 5 miles north-west of Tewkesbury. The name Ripple derives from the Norwegian 'Ripel', meaning a strip or tongue of land. Together with Uckinghall it lies to the east of the river Severn below Upton-on-Severn.

The first record of Ripple appears about AD 873, when it became a manor of the Bishop of Worcester, although evidence of Roman occupation has been found. The Village Cross stands at a meeting of ancient tracks from Bredon to Midsummer Hill, Malvern, and Worcester to Tewkesbury.

A battle during the Civil War was fought at Ripple in which eighty men died. General Waller, for the Parliamentarians, advanced from Tewkesbury towards Upton to fight the Royalist. Prince Maurice crossed Upton Bridge and routed Waller's troops, killing many and causing more to drown in the Severn while fleeing.

Churches of wood and stone had earlier stood on the site of the present church. The Norman church of St Mary was built about 1190–1195. Its great size (being 137 feet long) reflected the size of the manor of Ripple which then included Hill Croome, Earls Croome, Croome d'Abitot and parts of Upton, Holdfast and Queenhill. St Mary's church is chiefly noted for its fine misericordes which date from the 15th century and depict the seasonal activities on the land.

The churchyard contains the grave of the 'Village Giant', who died after mowing round the 100 acre Uckinghall Meadow in one day. His tombstone reads

'Ye who pass by behold my length
But never glory in your strength'.

Ripple, with Uckinghall, although a small village relatively unchanged in size over the years, can boast of a beautiful hall, old rectory, thatched cottages and black and white houses.

The Ashchurch to Malvern railway was built in 1862 and closed one hundred years later, victim to the Beeching Axe! In its heyday Ripple Station was busy with market garden produce, field peas and beans, milk and cattle being sent by train to Ashchurch and to Birmingham, as well as providing a passenger service to local towns.

The school, built in 1844 and closed in 1967, provided the local children with their education. The village hall, an ex-army hut, was erected in the early 1920s opposite the village pound. It has been the scene of many whist drives, dances, concerts, meetings, school dinners, and playgroup activities and is flourishing still.

Ripple, a century ago, presented a very different picture to the modern day. It was a hive of industry. There was a bakery, shop, brewery, laundry, blacksmith, shoemaker, butcher, mason, wheelwright and coal merchant, besides the numerous farmers and market gardeners. Very few people left the village to work, as the big houses, farms, railway and local industries employed most of the villagers. Many of the cottagers reared a pig in their back garden to help feed their large families. Today there is one pub and a shop. Most people leave the village to work in the towns, and the little cottages have changed out of all recognition to become very desirable residences.

Many houses in Uckinghall were at risk from flooding until the flood bank was built in 1976. Whilst making life extremely uncomfortable for those whose homes were under water, it proved an exciting time for the village children and always brought out the best in neighbourly help with boats ferrying people and goods wherever needed.

The face of the Ripple landscape will alter in 1989 when gravel extraction is due to start on 128 acres of river meadows. The gravel will be transported by barge to Worcester, so reducing the disturbance for the villagers. On completion of this long term project the company proposes to turn the site into a nature reserve. It is a relief to know that eventually rural peace will return to Ripple.

Rochford ✍

The name of the village is derived from its geographical position, where a ford crossing the river Teme gave access to the south side of the river over great flat slabs of sandstone rock which can be easily seen today. This rock ford has for centuries been under the fast flowing waters of the Teme as it makes its way from the mountains of Wales to join the Severn near Worcester, but nowadays when the river is low only horse riders have been seen crossing it. It is in a very important place, as on the south bank is the church of St Michael, a Norman church built in the early 12th century. Facing the river over a doorway is The Tree of Life, sadly now suffering from the elements.

Since May 1986 Rochford people have raised enough money to restore the church to perfect order, and surpassed the suggested price within six months of the money raising efforts. This alone is enough to tell you that the local people are thoughtful and caring, as are the former residents and friends of the village.

The school closed many years ago and the villagers have survived quite well with no public house! We rarely see more than the school bus nowadays as cars are owned and used to get to work which is often far from here. Once most people worked on the land, but modernisation has changed things and the seven remaining farms only need to employ ten men between them. Tenbury, the local market town, employs some residents and a few more work at the factories in Burford across the river from Tenbury.

To anyone passing through Rochford by car, look out on a straight piece of road for the green painted bus shelter. This wooden shelter faces a wonderful view of Clee Hill across in Shropshire, with farms showing the red clay soil on their ploughed fields, amongst the pretty patchwork of growing crops, deeply mellowed red brick farmhouses and buildings, and creeping up large modern lighter coloured cattle sheds. The river valley lies to the north of Rochford as does the boundary to Shropshire.

Spectacular views can be seen from the east end of the village at Hilltop Farm which overlooks the village as well as many more to the Welsh Mountains. Hilltop is 650 feet above sea level which is a good 300 feet

139

above the centre of the village and Hilltop Bank can cause troubles to motorists in winter time.

Past Rochfordians who made an imprint on local society include Morgan Edwards, retired farmer, whose instructions to many a Young Farmer regarding hedge laying and ploughing have proved most valuable with silver cups to prove it. Sydney Powell, Fred Yapp and Edward Keysell all farmed here in the 1960s, real hard-working farmers, who survived hard times in the 1930s. Bill Dipper, the pig-sticker who was renowned for 'doing a good job' in a wide area, could also thatch and invented his own corn dollies which he made as he rested in the shade after scything with a team a patch of corn. Mr Dipper's corn dollies have been preserved in a case in the church hall, donated by his family.

Village life may be thought of as mundane but there is a Church Fete each July and a Christmas Fayre near to Christmas and a party for the 60 children. There is still a community spirit in Rochford, villagers all feel concern for each other, and if in trouble help is soon at hand.

Rock

The name Rock comes from the old name 'aet ther ak', 'round the oak', but where the 'oak' was, nobody knows.

The village of Rock is situated in the north-west corner of Worcestershire. It is 600 feet above sea level at the highest point. Being so high there are wonderful views in every direction.

Rock church is the most outstanding building in the village. It is the largest of the Norman village churches in Worcestershire with fine examples of sculptured Norman arches.

In 1851, John Noake reported that no two habitations were within hailing distance of each other, except the cluster of cottages around the church. This is not so now. The village is quite compact, being all near the church and post office. It is only the village hall which is now left out on a limb.

It is said to be 'top coat colder' at Rock than anywhere else in Worcestershire and when one very old man from Rock was asked for the secret to his longevity he said that he had to live to a great age because it was too cold in the churchyard to go there!

Romsley 🪺

The garlic-filled glades of Romsley (from which it gets its name) were probably to be found in the ancient woodlands of the parish in the days of King Kenulph of Mercia, who died in AD 819.

About his seven year old son, Kenelm, arose a strongly believed in, though inaccurate, legend surrounding his kingship and murder. Of his body being buried under a thorn bush; of a dove dropping a scroll upon the high altar before the Pope in Rome, who in turn ordered a search to be made for the child – and many more details.

When Kenelm's body was found, and dug up, a strong spring of water with miraculous healing powers, welled up.

Today St Kenelm's church, containing architectural features of its 1000 years-plus of history, speaks of its legend origins. It is built over the sacred spot of the holy well in an extraordinary position, on a down-sloping, deep-sided valley. The spring today is diverted further down the hill.

Great numbers of pilgrims, attracted by the miracles of healing, journeyed to the village of Kenelmstowe which had arisen around the church.

With Henry VIII's Dissolution of the Monasteries, and later the building of the new Halesowen-Bromsgrove highroad, Kenelmstowe fell into ruins and the village of Romsley arose, close to the mobility of the new road.

Today the core of the village is by this main road, but village dwellings are also spread far and wide, within the parish, beside minor roads and lanes. One-time centrally placed fields are now in-filled with roads and houses.

It was customary, in the churchyard, on 17th July, the Feast Day of St Kenelm, to enjoy 'crabbing the parson', until the over-accurate, hard throwing of crab apples brought this high-spirited event to a close.

The now defunct Dayhouse Bank Methodist church is built on the site of a stable where John Wesley is supposed to have stabled his horse while missioning the nailers of Catshill.

The nearby Green Belt and Country Park attract walkers, horse riders and cars to the parish to enjoy the quiet and the fresh air.

Local and visiting patrons enjoy both drink and food at the Sun Inn and the Fighting Cocks.

Traditional local occupations could be summed up as farming, work at pubs and at industry in the Black Country; in domestic service and later at the Birmingham Sanatorium (now a block of flats), and at milling at Shut Mill between 1300 and 1886.

Today Romsley has become a village of commuters. Leyland Motors, Blue Bird Toffee Factory and the industrial Black Country are all providers of work. Locally about two thirds of the original farms still function, but with reduced labour. Shops, pubs and Romsley school also provide employment.

Rowney Green ✑

The village straggles across the top of a hill where every wind blows and all the rainbows end, just a road and a loop on a green ridge, but it has its own special enchantments. Climb the Holloway on a dark winter night, when the frost glitters under your feet and the crooked trees crowd in on you. Then you may feel like a Babe in the Wood haunted by shadows. But make your journey in late May-time, then the woods are different – magic with the scent of bluebells that drop down like a blue waterfall, to the secret places where the badgers make their homes. This is Peck Wood, a place of ancient oaks and bending birch trees. Or come in November when the air is full of smoke and noises, and stars and sparks fall on the tattered guy.

Come in summer when the Peace Hall is full of flowers, especially roses, nurtured by the Horticultural Society, the Flower Club and others. Or wander the village in spring to see gardens full of daffodils, snow-drops and flowering shrubs, while wild flowers lurk among the grasses. The Peace Hall sees a pageant of festivals as the year passes – Harvest Suppers, Christmas parties, birthday parties, wedding receptions, and so on. Dancing, singing, bellringing and drama go on all the year round.

As you leave the Peace Hall and continue along Rowney Green Lane you will catch sight of a picturesque old farmhouse. Rowney Green House Farm stands below you, tall and white, with a great green tree in front of it. Its neat rows of windows make it look like a giant dolls house dominating the countryside around it. Here in the great attic young folk danced as long ago as 1916. Beyond this farm lies Seechem's farmhouse which dates back to Tudor times. The earliest beginnings of Rowney Green (the name is derived from 'Rough Hay') probably lie buried here, not far from the old Roman Icknield Street. Behind Seechem lies Alcott Farm which stands on the oldest local site occupied since the Domesday

Book was compiled, and near the gate to Seechem, on Rowney Green Lane, stands picturesque Longfield Manor. It is thought a house has stood here since medieval times.

These homesteads show clearly that farming was and is a most important occupation in this area. A second important kind of work which has left its mark upon the landscape, was the gravel-working. One great site is now grown over with conifers and forms a Nature Conservation area. Another large gravel pit lies almost buried in foxgloves and brambles, whilst two white houses seem to keep guard over its mysterious depths.

But, more recently, a new industry has come to the village – The British Cast Iron Research Association, which hides its various buildings behind a tall screen of trees.

This is the way the jig-saw fits together to make a picture of Rowney Green, but some pieces are missing now. There is no post office, no telephone kiosk, no pub, no village shop, no school. The wooden church in the ancient wood is closed and silent among the bracken. There is no graveyard and so, no epitaphs, but there is a village still, and this high place is home.

Rubery 🦢

The earliest reference to Rubery occurs in the 16th century, showing the quarry and area as 'Rough Barrow' or 'Rowberrie'. Later it was Robery Hills and mentioned as part of the 'waste' of King's Norton Manor, probably meaning not inhabited or cultivated. A house, known as Rubery Farm, built in the 17th century, was later used as the vicarage for St Chad's church, until it was demolished in 1970. In the area were the hamlets of 'La Wetheye' now the Whetty, and 'Etchey' now Eachway and when they grew all became the village of Rubery. It lies between the Lickey Hills and the Waseley Hills with the well known 'wind gap' between, as anyone knows who crosses the by-pass by either of the bridges! The Callow Brook rises in the Waseley Hills and flows along the ridge and into the river Rea, in the grounds of Rubery Hill Hospital. This hospital was built as a Lunatic Asylum in 1882.

In the middle of the 18th century, the stage coach route from Birmingham to Bristol went up Rose Hill, Lickey, but the journey downhill was so steep that in 1831 an easier route was constructed, a new road. Now New Road is a thriving shopping centre. At the bottom of Rose Hill was a staging post called the Old Rose and Crown but when the new road was built so a new staging post was needed, hence the New Rose and Crown. There were four public houses, three of which had their own stabling, where farmers taking produce to Birmingham stopped to refresh themselves and rest their horses.

In the 17th century, nailmaking was the principal occupation and there is a pair of nailers' cottages still lived in, though modernised, in Holy Well Lane. Further down the lane is St Chad's Well, said to be the spot where St Chad rested on his walk-about. At the bottom of this lane is Chadwich Manor built in the 17th century. The Manor with 431 acres is now part of the National Trust and was given by the Cadbury family.

The Rubery Mission Church of St Chad was built in 1895 and took as its model a 15th century timber church. It was replaced in 1958 by a large modern one.

The population numbers about 12,000. Many work at 'Austins' Longbridge, some work at the Industrial Centre, and others in the vicinity. St Chad's Infant School is now a Community Centre and there are many and varied clubs for both sexes. There are several farms in the area, and a large Country Park, which is much enjoyed by young and old alike.

The river Rea rises on the north side of the Waseley Hills, where groups of school children love to search through the undergrowth in order to find the actual source. That area is the only claim Rubery has to a regal past, Anne Boleyn's parents owned Gannow Manor. Her father, Thomas, was an ambitious man and owned considerable property. There is not a lot left of the Manor, which has been excavated by students from Birmingham University. The area now is built on, though roads in the area are called Gannow, as is the school, and Boleyn.

Rushwick 🌾

To many, the village of Rushwick is just a name outside the city boundary, 2 miles west of Worcester Cross, on the road to Hereford. But delving into the past we learn that it was part of a large tract of land, the ancient Manor of Clopton. This was granted by King Offa of Mercia to Bishop Mildred in AD 775 and by the time of Domesday, 1086 – 'it was a flourishing community'.

Rushwick today is not a picturesque village, having no central green or church but the whole parish, which includes Upper Wick and Crown

The Old Dairy, Rushwick

East, bordered in the south by the river Teme, is pleasant farmland of former hopyards and fruit orchards with views to the south-west, 7 miles away, of the lovely line of the Malvern Hills.

The name Rushwick comes from the Danish 'Rysc Wic' meaning 'the dairy farm in the rushes' and certainly the flood-meadows beside the Teme were formerly marshlands. In Upper Wick, Wick Episcopi was the Bishop of Worcester's country house, mentioned in Domesday as being linked with Lower Wick. It is now a private house with a ha-ha.

Nearby Broadmore Green is a short lane containing a cluster of work buildings which served Crown East Court to the north. This is now Aymestrey Boys Preparatory School. An attractive half-timbered house was the dairy and another cottage was the bakery. These, and the laundry, are all still to be found. There was also a blacksmith, a wheelwright, a cider press and a saw pit.

Crown East, or Crow Nest, is the highest point of the parish. There was a chantry there in 1256 but it became disused. The present church of

St Thomas was originally built as a private chapel by the Bramwell family beside Crown East Court but it was moved and rebuilt on the main road to Bromyard and licenced for public worship on 26th October, 1876 by the Bishop of Worcester. Mr Bramwell also built a small school next to the church and it began with a dozen pupils in January, 1877. Children from Rushwick had to walk the mile to and from school right up to 1964 when a new Primary School opened in Upper Wick Lane. The old school building was sold and became a glove factory, now the last in Worcester.

Just a mile from the church towards Broadheath, but still in the church parish, Edward Elgar, the composer, was born in 1857; in later years he was to give violin lessons at Aymestrey School.

Inevitably, as a hybrid community, part-rural and part-urban, Rushwick needed a focal centre and this was found by the provision of a village hall. The first building used was a small wooden hut with a corrugated-iron roof. However, after the development of a large new housing estate in 1957, the need for a bigger hall became more urgent and, after 18 years of planning and fund-raising, the new Rushwick Village Hall was built on the western fringe of the village.

So 'the flourishing community' of Domesday continues in a modern way – proud to support a thriving post office and general store, a second village shop and two farm shops, a primary school, a village hall, an inn and a church (with no signs of closing down).

St Michael's

At Worcestershire's most westerly tip, close to the point where the county meets its neighbours Shropshire and Herefordshire, lies the village of St Michael's.

Visitors to the area, climbing upwards from the market town of Tenbury Wells, will glimpse the very reason for the village's existence – St Michael's church and College – as they cross the broad expanse of Oldwood Common.

The Gothic-style choir school and church, complete with its famous 4-manual Willis organ, were founded in 1856 by Sir Fredrick Arthur Gore Ousley and, in the same year, the church was consecrated to form the parish of St Michael's, taking in parts of Tenbury, Leysters and Middleton.

Although exact records are difficult to find, it is thought that the population of the village has increased somewhat since the turn of the century. What is certain is the fact that many changes have taken place in recent years.

The village school, retaining its lantern ventilators and stone mullion windows, has long since been converted into a private house, as has the old blacksmith's shop, the Methodist chapel, and the local tuck shop, although the original owner did subsequently celebrate her 100th birthday.

Despite these and many other changes which have taken place in the 130 years or so since its formation, the village still has a thriving community which supports many activities – religious, social, and sporting – that revolve around the church, the hall and the pub, plus its very own Parish Magazine published every month.

Unfortunately, the reason for the village's formation all those years ago, St Michael's College, closed in 1985. However, its magnificent church is still used and maintained by the 290-strong and growing local population.

The parish hall, originally an army hut sited on Oldwood Common, was in 1942 moved to a site in the centre of the village and is the venue for many activities, ranging from monthly WI meetings through to Harvest Festivals and other celebrations.

Local business is also thriving. Although still mainly agriculturally based, other enterprises include parsley growing and drying, race horse training, a tree nursery, and the latest venture – the conversion of an old mill into a residential country club complete with game fishing and golf – augurs well for the future prosperity of the village.

The village has always had its characters, and stories about both people and places still abound, even if they do appear to exaggerate with time. Who would believe, for example, that a house on the edge of Oldwood Common acquired its name 'The Lion's Den' because years ago it was used as the restplace for a travelling circus and that its cellars were used to accommodate the lions during their stay. How about the connotation behind a house named 'The Shrouds'? Even today on a dull autumn or winter's morning, for some inexplicable reason, it still seems to attract an eerie cloak of mist.

It is also difficult to imagine a local Methodist preacher not only organising whist drives and dances, but also on occasions entertaining the locals with his 'donkey braying act'. Or how about the spinster who, in her best Sunday dress complete with large flowered hat, rode through the village every week on her bicycle trailing a lawn mower behind her, so that she could trim the grass around one particular grave in the churchyard!

Salwarpe 🌿

Seal warpen, Salu warpen, Sal warpen, choose which one you will, the pleasantest derivation is 'by the twisted willow'.

Salwarpe village today stands almost on an island between the river Salwarpe and the Droitwich canal. With her 14th century church built on an older foundation, there is mention of Salwarpe in an old Saxon document of about AD 770. Salwarpe Court, once a single storied manor house, the birthplace of one of the Earls of Warwick and later endowed to Catherine of Aragon as part of her marriage settlement at the time of her marriage to the ill-fated Prince Arthur, still stands serenely in the sunlight. The present owner is replacing the white plaster with mellow brickwork, painstakingly and correctly restoring the Elizabethan herring-bone style. The church cottages, once a school then a shop, still face the lychgate and their gardens slope gently down to Brindley's canal, built to take salt down to the river Severn. The Old Mill House, mentioned in the Domesday Book, dreams above the mill stream which is still a rendez-vous for young lovers, as it has been throughout the centuries.

But Salwarpe is not just a memorial to the past. The great barns of Salwarpe Court have been converted into luxury homes, bringing new families into the village. The Old School House is now a high technology workshop. Salwarpe House, once the old rectory, has several young people sharing flats. Churchfield Farm is the home of a busy, farming family. A new village hall brings hundreds of people on various occasions throughout the year. The WI is growing and, best of all, the solid, square, no-nonsense tower of the church of St Michael and All Angels looks down on busy paths that lead walkers, fishermen, boat people and regular worshippers to the Sunday Services. There is a Neighbourhood Watch, a Salwarpe Events Committee, a Village Hall Committee, a Parochial Church Council and a Parish Council. Salwarpe is alive and well and living in the 20th century!

It is very wet in Salwarpe. Low-lying and bordered on one side by the river and with the canal winding between the church and the Court, winter mornings can be dank and misty and the trees grow tall in the churchyard sheltering rooks, starlings, nuthatch and tree-creeper. The cedars of Salwarpe were imported from Malawi by a member of the Douglas family, one-time missionary and rector. They act as a 'high-rise' development with a lonely owl an occasional visitor and the other birds slotting in at different levels among the thick, dark, evergreen foliage.

On the canal, life abounds and long-tailed tits and reed warblers rustle and flit among the rushes. The Droitwich Canal Trust have dredged and cleared the canal from Droitwich to Ladywood Lock and, in the summer, the narrow boat, *Sabrina*, painted in the traditional green with roses, chugs her slow way from the Basin to Ladywood and back. When the canal fell into disuse some 20 years ago residents remember walking through it, in different places. Now two families keep small craft on it and spend happy hours just 'messing about in boats'.

For the imaginative there are certainly ghosts in Salwarpe. When the mists swirl over the weir surely a carriage passes from distant High Park, over the river, to the church? A clatter of horses' hooves down the lane and one expects to see a company of Yorkists, with swirling cloaks, rendezvousing at the Court. In the moonlight, among the quiet church-yard paths, one can imagine the whispering figures of monks, patiently pacing to and fro. And what of those 'Constables and Tithingmen' of Salwarpe who were so peremptorily bidden by their King to bring spades, shovels and pick axes on Monday morning at 5 o'clock, in August 1651, to work at the fortifications of Worcester City? (The original Command was found in the church and a facsimile of the letter hangs there still.)

The Shelsleys

Probably more people lose their way in The Shelsleys than in any other part of the county, for although Shelsley Walsh is world-famous for its Hill Climb, the hamlets of Shelsley Beauchamp and Shelsley Kings are scattered in a hidden valley of the river Teme running north to south between the towering heights of Woodbury Hill and Clifton Ridge.

The steep, narrow lanes of this valley, the wooded hillsides, the remote dwellings, the old hopyards, the cherry and apple orchards, together with the distant views of the Malvern and Clee Hills give a wonderful peace and a sense of isolation from the world of today. But on four days a year, people from all nations travel to Shelsley Walsh to take part in the world's oldest motoring Speed Event which was established on a farm track at the Court House in 1905 by The Midland Automobile Club, a track which is now tarmacadamed enabling drivers to achieve faster and faster times over the course. Raymond Mays made the Best Time of Day 21 times altogether and there is a memorial to him at the starting point.

Near the Hill Climb and the Court House, which dates from the time of Elizabeth I and was the home of the Walshes who were concerned in the capture of conspirators during the Gunpowder Plot, there stands the tiny church of St Andrew. The secluded position, the screenwork, the carved roof beam, wooden tomb, medieval window and star painted ceiling are some of the features which make this little 12th century church one of the loveliest in the county. It is built from tufa stone, or travertine of a rough spongy appearance which was quarried from nearby Southstone Rock, a limestone crag built up from the deposit of the stream running down to the river Teme.

Across the river at Shelsley Beauchamp there is the church of All Saints which stands close to farm buildings and has a 15th century tower and interesting font, sanctuary and chests.

In such a sheltered and hidden place as The Shelsleys there are of course many legends such as the haunting of Court House by a Lady Lightfoot who was imprisoned by her husband, subsequently murdered by him and whose ghost is said to drive a coach and four around the landing, down into the hall and into the lake behind the house. Witchery Hole, above the river on the hillside, is said to be a place where witches were burned in medieval times and where now there is a spot in which nothing can be grown. Just below Witchery Hole in West Mill Cottage, a door refuses to close despite locks and bolts. Strangers here, having at last discovered the beauties of The Shelsleys, might, after they had felt the ghostly although not unfriendly presence, feel tempted to leave the place in a hurry!

Shrawley ✣

Shrawley is an attractive small village with a character peculiarly its own, which is, perhaps, a reflection of its geographical location. Set in undulating countryside it is bounded by water on three sides and whoever wants either to enter or leave the village must first negotiate a steep descent to the valleys of Dick Brook (probably the first canalised brook in England) and Shrawley Brook and an equally steep ascent to the neighbouring parishes of Astley and Holt.

Traditionally, there was always great rivalry between Shrawley's young men and their neighbours including those in Ombersley across the other waterway – the river Severn. Perhaps the advent of the motor-car has changed this rather insular outlook, for village fights are no longer a part of everyday life!

The suffix 'ley' in Shrawley is shared by many neighbouring villages and denotes a wooded area. Shrawley Wood suffers from the lack of historical documentation which affects the rest of the village – no Domesday entry, alas – but it is probable that parts of it are some 7000 years old. Shrawley people are proud of the fact that oaks from Shrawley Wood were used to repair the Houses of Parliament after bomb damage sustained during the Second World War.

The whole wood formed part of the Shrawley Wood House Estate, but now roughly half is managed by the Forestry Commission. There are many lovely walks through the woods, leading down to the river meadows which extend along to the Lenchford Hotel. The two main entrances are opposite the Rose and Crown and the New Inn respectively. At the Lenchford end the wood rises in a steep escarpment where remains may be seen of an old cave known locally as Rock Seat. The Anglo-Saxon word for a cave probably formed the first syllable of the village's name. From Rock Seat tradition has it that hermits used to rescue unwanted babies who had been set adrift higher up the Severn at Bewdley. These were educated by the hermits and given the surname Severn.

Another interesting area in the wood will presumably never become the subject of legend for the facts are well-documented. Summer Cottage overlooking the Middle Pool, was a favourite spot for the Vernon family who had owned the estate for 300 years. It is a ruin now, but a tomb marks the grave of Sir George Vernon who, after falling out with the Church during the Tithe War of the early 1930s, expressed his wish to be buried there rather than in consecrated ground 'by prating priests'.

The Wood House Park is the setting for the Village Fete, which always takes place on the Saturday of the August Bank Holiday. This is an event which draws all the village in to help, proceeds going to the upkeep of the church and the village hall, which is the former school. The school closed in 1977 and was bought by the village and opened in 1984 as the village hall.

The church of St Mary celebrated its 9th Centenary in 1982, but was closed for repairs in 1985 as the south wall of the chancel was moving outwards and causing concern over the safety of the roof. After mammoth efforts by the 400 inhabitants most of the £26,000 needed has been raised and the church re-opened in 1987 in time for Midnight Mass on Christmas Eve, though some work still remains to be done. The priest-in-charge now has four parishes in his care, though the rectory is in Shrawley.

Physically the village has changed little since the war, with relatively few new houses having been built, though of the 14 council houses, only 3 now remain council property. The original houses are a blend of black and white timber frame and the later mellow red brick which echoes the red sandstone which surfaces in many parts of Shrawley, dictating the route of the main road from Worcester to Stourport.

Sidemoor 🦋

Sidemoor was once a village surrounded by marshland and fields. The village consisted of a handful of cottages and during the 18th and 19th centuries the occupants were engaged in the major industry of that time, namely, the making of nails, the origins of which are not known exactly. Though now swallowed up by Bromsgrove, Sidemoor still retains a lively sense of a village community.

Nailmaking was a hard trade involving whole families, including the children, some very young, and as families were large in those days it could number anything up to 15, 16 and perhaps more. The cottages they lived in had one room upstairs and one down, most probably rented from the Nailmaster. There was an outbuilding attached to the cottage which contained a furnace and the equipment for the making of nails, which they called the nail shop. The family spent their days in this nail shop working long hours making different types of nails using material bought from the Nailmaster, as was the fuel for the furnace.

The 19th century saw the start of strikes by the nailmakers for better pay and conditions. The local cavalry was usually used to break up the strike meetings, but the nailers had their own method to quell these charges, they made a nail called the 'tis-was', a four spiked nail, one spike of which always landed upwards, and this was thrown under the hooves of the horses.

There was no church in the village at this time and church meetings were held in the cottages which most villagers attended. Eventually in 1838 a group of church people got together to build a small stone chapel and this became the focal point of the village; as the years passed the stone chapel was replaced by others, there is still a church in Sidemoor today.

One of the earliest cotton mills was started in Sidemoor in the Middle Ages. It was one of two of the earliest cotton spinning factories and one of the first mills to install a steam engine. It is believed that in the early 1820s Benjamin Sanders of Bromsgrove took possession of the then disused Sidemoor Mill for the purpose of manufacturing buttons, particularly the cloth covered type. The factory was extended in 1829 and by 1830 there were 300 employees, mostly women, who were paid one shilling and one penny per day. In 1915 the factory was burnt down leaving one small part of the original late 18th century mill. The building was restored and is still in existence today and has been run by four generations of the Nicholls family who took over the business and who still trade under the name of Benjamin Sanders. Button making at the factory was discontinued some five years ago and between 50 and 60 people are at present employed still making badges.

More recent years have seen Sidemoor as a thriving market garden area, a great number of allotments producing a variety of vegetables and fruit, particularly strawberries, which were taken to local and Birmingham markets for sale. Unfortunately the market garden industry has dwindled in the last few years especially with the introduction of the 'pick your own' type of farms.

Spetchley ✿

A scattered area, dominated by Spetchley Park, home of the Berkeley family for some 500 years and where the gardens and deer park are regularly open to visitors.

The name comes from the Low Hill meeting place of the Oswaldslow Hundred, which was an area east of Worcester, an old division of lands.

The church contains some interesting monuments. One (to Rowland Berkeley and his wife) is a particularly good example of early 17th century alabaster work.

Stoke Prior ✿

Stoke Prior made its first appearance in history as a hunting lodge in the Forest of Feckenham, frequented by King John. The church dates from this period and has a 13th century tower which must be one of the most beautiful in England. The church itself was restored in the 19th century by the famous architect, J. R. Pearson, designer of Truro cathedral, who was also an amateur blacksmith and whose wrought iron can be seen on the font cover and the south door.

153

The village nowadays is very scattered and includes on its borders the hamlets of Wychbold, Upton Warren, Puddle Wharf and Stoke Heath.

Salt had been mined at Droitwich since before Roman times, but in the 1850s an engineer, John Corbett, discovered a method of extracting it by digging a shaft down to the seam, pouring in water and pumping out the brine to deposit the salt. By this means he made a huge fortune. He built good houses for his workers and assisted in many philanthropic enterprises.

The chimney of his factory was the third tallest in England until in 1930 95 feet was lopped off the top of it. The claim of Stoke Prior to tall buildings was however restored in the same year when the BBC built its radio station on the edge of the village with two masts, each 700 feet high – quite the tallest buildings, then as now.

The AI Centre in Sugarbrook was one of the first in the country to pioneer the artificial insemination of cattle and now has a world-wide reputation.

In the 1950s an ancient house in Bromsgrove High Street had to be demolished in a road-widening scheme. It was taken down and rebuilt, piece by numbered piece, at a site at Avoncroft College on Stoke Heath. The reconstructed town house became the nucleus of a Museum of Buildings, the first of many such in England.

In Shaw Lane, at the point where the river Spadesbourne leaves the village, on the site of an old watermill, the Boxfoldia Company had built a large factory and warehouse. This had been derelict and for sale for many years when in 1935 a young brushmaker from Stirchley purchased it. His name was Leslie Harris – and he was immediately successful, soon building himself a splendid new factory in the Hanbury Road, from which his paint brushes have been exported all over the world. To provide hardwood for his brush handles he planted areas of woodland near his factory and these coppices are now a pleasant feature of the local landscape.

The village is traversed by the Birmingham–Worcester canal built in the 18th century for the transport of coal, stone and of course salt. It is now mainly used for leisure activities. Its flight of 36 locks from Stoke Pound to Tardebigge tunnel is the longest in England. At Sugarbrook, where the lane passes over the canal, long before the canal was cut, there was a pub called the Blacksmith's Arms. After Queen Victoria came to the throne it was re-named the Queen's Head, but it was still the site of a blacksmith's smithy. The last smith to work there, from 1920 to 1970 was Jack Bennett. This pub, the Queen's Head, is now a fully-licensed restaurant, catering mainly for the pleasure-boat trade.

Stoke Works ❧

A village which has been transformed from an early Victorian industrial site to a pleasant modern area and all in the last 30 years. The long main street is set with wide grass verges and with the canal running parallel with it.

On the opposite side is the railway line, just out of sight. Two inns, the Boat & Railway – well named – and at the other end of the village is the Butcher's Arms, and the shop.

Until about 30 years ago most residents worked at the saltworks nearby and lived in rows of typical industrial cottages, one of which was a terrace of about 60 cottages, conjoined but with a few entries as a back approach. There were also other shorter rows across the road. All these have been demolished to make way for modern houses, except the very large school still displaying the Corbett arms – a raven – and a clock permanently at 5.45. This building is now used for industrial purposes, as also is the village hall built about 1925.

Stoke chimney, at the saltworks, was a Worcestershire landmark but demolished in the early 1950s. Now however, there is another landmark, the BBC masts at Wychbold only a mile away. When lit up at night, they are visible from many miles away. A veritable 'Pillar of Fire by Night' indeed.

Stone ❧

The hamlet of Stone is situated on the A448 road 2 miles south from Kidderminster to Bromsgrove. At the top of Stone Hill stands the lovely ancient church of St Mary, with the vicarage nearby. There is the black and white parish room and school house. The village school was former- ly small and primitive but now enlarged and modernised is a thriving C of E First School. A few large houses stand nearby and a farm house and farm buildings. Council houses and bungalows are in the area.

About a mile up the road is a roundabout, a junction of roads leading west to Worcester, and Stourbridge to the east.

Mustow Green was a quiet hamlet until recently when traffic was diverted through from the M5. There is a large garage. Otherwise it is a pleasant healthy place to live with beautiful surrounding scenery. The name is derived from 'muster' – as troops 'mustered' on the village green during the Civil War. There is a lane called Red Lane which it is said 'ran with blood' during the fighting.

Another quiet hamlet, Shenstone, lies to the west with farmland and country houses, a shop and a public house. To the east is the hamlet of Harvington where there stands the Dairy Stores, the post office, and also the Talbot Inn and a cluster of houses. The old smithy is now a busy engineering business, near a lane leading to Harvington Hall. This is an Elizabethan manor house surrounded by a moat, famous for its architecture and built about 1580. There are several skilfully constructed hiding places where priests took refuge during days of religious persecution. Since recent renovation, many tourists are attracted to this interesting old Worcestershire treasure, a mecca for Catholics.

On the main road stands the Stone and District Festival Hall, a meeting place and home for a wide variety of activities. It was built during the Second World War as a hostel for Land Army girls, and later to house German prisoners. There are three or four flats adjoining the Hall.

Stone is a delightful rural area which has much interesting early history. It is still in the Green Belt.

Storridge ✑

Storridge, a small hamlet, is situated midway between Hereford and Worcester with the river Rumble running through the picturesque countryside.

The river Severn was the main highway for the area as there were few roads. The upland alternative which avoided the forest of marshland was the natural ridgeway from the Abberley Hills running southwards through Storridge or Stony Ridge as it was then known and over Whitmans hill to Malvern and from there to the Forest of Dean – this was part of the Droitwich salt route.

In 1351 wine was being brewed for ecclesiastical purposes. The name Vinesend is still on the map and vines are still being grown in the Storridge area. Coal was also found there but the mines were never worked as the gentry bought up the land to prevent this. Coal was delivered to the wealthy by Wilesmiths of Malvern while the poor collected theirs from Malvern Link railway yard, a distance of some 4 miles.

From 1397 to 1400 there are written records of the local 'witch' who is still talked about. Her name was Amisia Daniel and she lived in a hovel at

156

Wild Goose Hill where she was known as the old gander and preferred pigs for company.

The year of 1843 saw a Malvern builder, George Cann, supplying stone for the railway line between Worcester and Hereford from the quarries which are still worked at Storridge. He also built Storridge church in 1854 which was paid for by the rector of Cradley, enabling the Storridge people to attend services without the long trek to Cradley.

In 1929 the local people all went to see the Holy Thorn at the Grittlesend at the old Christmas time of January 6th. The Holy Thorn still stands and is said to be an offshoot of the Glastonbury Thorn and to burst into flower at Christmas Eve at midnight.

The parish of Storridge is rural and is very scattered. It used to have a number of hopyards and as soon as September came a string of gipsy caravans wound its way along the lanes, the people coming from the Midlands and earning enough money for warm clothes for the winter. Alas this is no more and although Storridge is essentially a farming community, this is taken up with dairy farms and 'pick-your-own' fruit farms.

Crumpton Hill, a small corner of the parish, used to be called Cromwell's Hill and it was at Hill Farm that Cromwell mustered his troops before the Battle of Worcester.

If one crosses the main Worcester Road from Crumpton Hill, one reaches Birchwood, again all in the parish of Storridge. It was at Birchwood Lodge that Sir Edward Elgar, the composer, lived for many years. The wonderful views over the whole of Worcestershire may have inspired some of his music.

Stoulton ✣

Stoulton village is a scattered collection of hamlets around the A44 between Whittington and Drakes Broughton. Part of the village is on a hill, and the name is said to mean: 'Place on a hill' or 'Place of a throne'. Southwards is Hawbridge with Claverton estate, and The Bird in Hand. Southeast lie Windmill Hill, and houses and farms on the road to Egdon and the Berkeley Arms. The village was part of Eastnor Castle Estate until 1917.

There are a number of interesting buildings. The church and font are Norman. The church tower was rebuilt in 1936 and the bells recast with a grant from Hamilton Bruce Kingsford, a banker from Cheltenham, in memory of his father, the much respected vicar. Carved panelling behind the altar and stained glass windows removed from St Helen's, Worcester, were donated by members of the Kingsford family. The woman spinning in one window is a portrait of Rev Kingsford's daughter, Madelaine Chaytor.

Manor Farm is a 17th century farmhouse with later additions. The farm was sold to a developer, and large urban houses are replacing the farm buildings, apart from the old barn which is being converted. It had an unusual horse weathervane which has been removed to Allesborough Farm, Pershore.

The old vicarage is 17th century, and was enlarged around 1820 with material from a tithe barn to accommodate the incumbent's 13 children.

The old school house was once lived in by Gustav Holst's half-brother, who played the cello, and taught music in local schools.

The village school was opened in 1877 with funds contributed by Earl Somers and the parishioners. In 1933 the school was closed; and in 1967, the Parochial Church Council and Parish Council drew up a Trust Deed providing for the use of the hall by people of the parish, with a Management Committee. Annual events are a flower show, dog show, Harvest Supper and Christmas Dinner. The church fete is held on alternate years at Breach Farm.

The Mount was a posting house on the London Road. Several windows were bricked up in the days of window tax. These have recently been reopened. A yearly Wake was held outside the inn, with stalls, backsword play and shin kicking. The landlord presented copper kettles as prizes.

Across the A44 is Froggery Lane, so called after the shoeing of horses hooves or frogs. The old forge house, a thatched cruck cottage, is lived in, though the forge no longer functions.

In the churchyard are tombstones to the Hemus and Blizard families. They left a charity to supply loaves of bread for the villagers. People remember these being distributed until the days of wartime food rationing. The yearly interest of £5-6 is now given to people who have served the Church or community.

The village shopkeeper and postmistress, Mrs Merriman, a fit 93, had cooked for Stanley Baldwin and Rudyard Kipling. She worked at the post office in the Old Brew House for 46 years. It had been a post office since 1854. She also sang in the church choir for 60 years. Shop and post office have gone, along with the school, forge and orchards; and are replaced by private houses and a Honda Garage.

158

Stourton 🦫

Stourton lies in the green belt adjacent to the West Midlands conurbation. The approach from the industrial Black Country is a wide road, the A458, with houses nestling among the woods; on the other side, there are views across unbroken countryside to the far Malvern Hills. Today the scene is threatened by the shadow of a proposed West Midlands Orbital Motorway.

Ask anyone for directions to Stourton and they begin by mentioning the Stewponey Hotel. A strange sounding name with many equally strange derivations. The most colourful being that the inn was started by a soldier who, whilst serving in the Peninsular Wars (1808–14), married a girl from Estapona, a village near Gibraltar. On returning home he named his tavern thus, but drinkers, who came from all around, quickly changed it to Stewponey. A painting of the girl from Estapona still hangs there today. Another more likely source is that the name was taken from the nearby 'Stewri-Pons' where horses were tethered and watered. A tale is told of an unfortunate traveller, carousing at the tavern, who drowned whilst trying to rescue his horse which had fallen in the water. Fact or folklore? We shall never know.

Nearby is imposing Stourton Castle. It nestles by the side of the river Stour, which formed part of the moat. The castle was built in 1110, and was used as a hunting lodge by King John as it was surrounded by dense forest. Mary Queen of Scots spent part of her childhood here and in 1500 Cardinal Pole was born here and this room is still preserved. The great door remains but was greatly damaged by cannon balls in the Civil War. It is recorded that De Grezbrook, a royalist knight, returned exceedingly angry to the castle after battle and Prince Rupert called him the 'Angry Bear'. Ever since a bear has been the symbol of Stourton Castle and a plaster cast of a bear hangs on a wall of the baronial hall.

Another notable building is Prestwood House dating back to the time of King John who visited the estate several times between 1200 – 1210. In 1921 it became the property of the Staffordshire, Wolverhampton and Dudley Joint Committee and was used as a sanatorium for the treatment of pulmonary tuberculosis. Prestwood House was converted to a nurses home and administration block but was sadly reduced to ruins by a fire in January 1922 then later rebuilt. The hospital closed in 1985. Today the house is used as a private nursing home for the elderly with further developments planned. A small sandstone building nearby, now the

159

Stourton Castle

daughter church of St Peter's, Kinver, also served as a school for young children.

The name Stourton comes from a 'ton' – a fenced enclosure – on the river Stour, a small, meandering river used both for trade and pleasure. The trade was mainly the iron trade. Water was needed to power the machinery for the slitting mills. In 1662 there were plans to make the Stour navigable from Bristol to Stourbridge to transport coal but this never materialised. The Stour remained, as it still is today, a quiet retreat for the fisherman and the gentle stroller.

Thus the roads became of paramount importance. The turnpike road between Bristol and Chester, now the A449, was a never ending line of wagons and carts carrying iron, glass, pottery and textiles. Crossing from east to west came the Bridgnorth turnpike road. In May 1772 the Staffordshire and Worcestershire canal was opened, followed by the Stourbridge and Dudley canal in 1779. Today narrow boats tie up at Stourton locks.

Stourton has had its share of high drama. This is commemorated in the names Gibbet Lane and Gibbet Wood. In 1812 a Mr Ben Robins was murdered and robbed on his way home from Stourbridge. The assailant was captured by clever detective work by the 'Bow Street Runners', tried, convicted and executed at Stafford and his body strung up on a 'gibbet' at the scene of his crime. It is said that hundreds of people flocked to the spot to view this gruesome spectacle. He was the last murderer to be strung up on a gibbet in the Midlands.

Strensham ꙮ

'Strensham? Isn't that where the Service Area is?' ask strangers, but few know of its historic past.

The church contains a variety of elaborate memorials to the Russells, who owned the manor for four centuries and were influential locally and nationally. St John the Baptist church stands high up overlooking the Avon and from it there are spectacular views of May Hill, Bredon Hill and the Malverns. From its position, Strensham got its name of Strengisho in 972, which meant 'Strong Hill'. Inside the church is a rare painted medieval rood screen, now fronting the gallery, but unfortunately the 23 panels depicting saints were repainted in Victorian times, and only Christ on the centre panel was untouched. Among the ornate alabaster monuments to the Russells in the chancel, there are several brasses, one of which dates from 1375, and is the oldest figure brass in Worcestershire. By its side is another, in memory of Sir John Russell who was Master of the Horse to Richard II and who died in 1405. He was granted a licence to crenellate his house and Strensham had a castle from then until the Civil War; indeed, the three principal garrisons in the area were said to be Tewkesbury, Evesham and Strensham. The moat of the castle still remains behind Moat Farm.

Sir William Russell was the Governor of Worcester at the time of the Civil War, and took such a significant part in the Royalist cause that his castle was 'pillaged to the bare walls' and his 'estate wasted'. However, the moat of the castle still remains behind Moat Farm.

At the time of the Restoration, *Hudibras* became enormously popular. It was written by Samuel Butler who was born in Strensham in 1612.

In 1697, Sir Francis Russell founded the Almshouses and endowed them with rent charges on land from as far away as Chipping Camden. His wife gave the means for the schooling of '12 poor children – to learn to read, to knit, and to say the Church Catechism'.

John Taylor purchased the estate in 1815. He was a Sheriff of Worcester and a man of great wealth. He knocked down the family seat of the Russells and built himself a splendid mansion, Strensham Court. He made a lake, to improve the view and he and his successors built farms and houses extensively. The derelict Court was finally destroyed by fire after the last owners left in 1935.

In the 1950s Coventry Water Works built a pumping station and filter beds near the Avon and, at that time, electricity was brought to the village. The greatest change, however, came when the M5 and the M50 sliced their way through Strensham. The Service Area not only gave employment to some inhabitants, but also made Strensham a familiar name to motorists.

The Almshouses, founded by Sir Francis Russell in 1697, fell into decay after the last residents left in the 1950s, and it was only in 1987 that, at last, they were restored. Now three modern houses are occupied to replace the six humble 'one up and one down' dwellings, which had a pump in the yard and a privy up the garden.

Considerable building has taken place in the village in recent years, and more is in the planning stage. The Court Stables have recently been converted into 12 stylish homes. The village hall has been rebuilt by some energetic residents and the mill now has 40 moorings on the Avon. Few people now work in the village, although there are still four farms, growing mostly arable crops, or raising beef cattle. Most inhabitants commute to surrounding towns or a few speed up the motorway to Birmingham. Strensham looks as if it should thrive therefore, even if its future does not quite match its illustrious past.

Tardebigge 🦑

Tardebigge is not a village, but one of several hamlets in the parish of Tutnall and Cobley. This parish once formed the area of Bordesley Abbey and, with the church, was once partly in Worcestershire and partly in Warwickshire. In 1774 the boundary line, which went through the church, was altered in Worcestershire's favour.

Tardebigge may not be a village in the true sense of the word, but around the church of St Bartholomew is the heart of this ancient place. There has been a place of worship here for over a thousand years; the present church stands on a swelling hill and, like its predecessors, provides a well-loved and notable landmark to all the country around. From the church itself, and from all the vantage points on the hill, there are extensive and varied views of the Clees, the Clents, the Malverns, and even further.

Near to the church stands Tardebigge C of E School and this was

162

Lock gates at Tardebigge

started by the Plymouth family who lived at nearby Hewell Grange (now a Youth Custody Centre and owned by HM Prisons). In the 1820s the Plymouth family closed the Magpie Inn, which stood on the site of the present school, and installed a schoolmaster and his wife. The Inn had previously been in the hands of the Hemmings family for over 200 years and the Bromsgrove Court Leet used to meet in this house during the years 1817–1820. But now a Mr and Mrs Turner taught the boys and girls the three 'Rs' and the Bible.

In the churchyard there used to be an offshoot of the Glastonbury Thorn, which has been known to bloom at Christmas, and on the edge of the hill, which slopes down to the Worcester and Birmingham Canal, there are accounts of a spring with curative powers, but this has ceased to run and there are no remains.

Within a close radius of the church are scattered farms, High House, Dial House, Patchetts, Sheltwood and many others, all with a long history of service to the land. The fields are now mainly grazed and there is some cereal growing but, until a few years ago, the nearby views would have been dominated by flourishing orchards.

Below the church an ancient path leads down to the canal, Tardebigge Tunnel and the 58 locks descending to Worcester. Here also are the buildings and cottages of the New Wharf which came into being with the building of this part of the canal in the 19th century. Cottages, workshops, an old mill, and traditional narrowboats form a picturesque scene, quiet in the winter, but busy in the summer with passing boats and towpath walkers.

Towards Hewell Grange is 'The Tardebigge' which has, of late, had a chequered history. It was once the Tardebigge village hall, built in 1911, a magnificent concept where local people could enjoy a library, craft and educational classes, cricket, bowls and a weekly bath for a penny. All this was provided through the forethought and generosity of the Plymouth family but, alas, with the breaking up of the Estate, Tardebigge lost its village hall.

Throckmorton

Named from a Warwickshire family, the village has a 13th century church approached from a cattle grid into fields. A moat behind the church is believed to mark the site of the old manor house of the Throckmorton family.

Tibberton

Tibberton is situated about 5 miles from Worcester and 4 miles from Droitwich. The Birmingham–Worcester canal runs to the north of the village, Birmingham–Bristol railway line is to the east and the M5 motorway to the west. Since the building of the M5 and a junction some 1½ miles from the village there have been a considerable number of new houses built and the population now stands at about 600, many of whom commute daily to Birmingham.

Tibberton is still fortunate to have a post office/village store, there are six farms, two smallholdings, a thriving village school and two public houses. There were originally two forges and until recently a farrier also lived in the village.

The church is situated some ¾ mile from the centre and is dedicated to St Peter ad Vincula and was rebuilt in 1868, replacing the original which was built around the 13th century.

There are still members of the Tandy family living in Tibberton today whose ancestors were mentioned in the Domesday Book and a story was recorded in 1718 of a Roger Tandy who lived during the reign of King James I . . . 'whilst he was at Sir John Packington's at Westwood Park, he demonstrated his strength for a wager. He took up a hogshead full of beer and after drinking from the bunghole he set it down again. All this by the strength of his arms without resting it on his knees or elsewhere!'

The present landlady of the Bridge Inn was a Tandy and she took over from her parents who kept the Inn before her.

The other inn situated in the village is Speed the Plough where it is reputed the infamous Oddingley murders were planned in 1806.

Evelench and Ravenshill farms have many historical attributes. Evelench at one time belonged to the Winter family who were noted for their connections with the famous Gunpowder Plot and at Ravenshill, King Canute was supposed to have resided towards the latter part of his reign and fought battles against the Saxons in Worcestershire.

Coming now to the present day Tibberton, it can be said that in spite of its growth it still maintains a 'village' atmosphere and many activities take place in the village hall which is situated in the centre. There is a Brownie pack, Keep Fit, club for mothers with under 5 year olds, Tibberton singers and a very friendly WI, so whatever your age or interest there is something for everyone.

In the summer months there is almost a holiday atmosphere prevailing as many holiday-makers of all nationalities on canal barges make Tibberton a 'stop-over' and can be seen exploring the village or just enjoying a bite and a pint in the gardens of the Bridge Inn and Speed the Plough. The canal is also a favourite venue of the Birmingham Angling Association who hold fishing competitions during the summer months.

Naturally Tibberton has progressed with the times and enjoys all the 'mod-cons' which have been introduced over the years: electricity, water, sewerage, even a 40 mph speed limit and also the benefits from many services brought into the village from a mobile library, a milkman, butcher and baker, to fresh fish from Grimsby, and a daily bus service to Worcester.

Trimpley

Trimpley village is located high above the east side of the Severn Valley.

Holy Trinity, Trimpley, is a chapel of ease to St Mary and All Saints, Kidderminster and was dedicated to the Virgin Mary. The present church was consecrated on 2nd August, 1844, by Bishop Pepys. The site and materials were given by Joseph Chillingworth who also gave an endowment for the church fabric. It is built in the Norman style, seating about 120 people. Nave and chancel are one, apse, bellcote all neo-Norman. The facade is ornate with the west portal arcading above a rose window and a bellcote.

A short distance from the church lies a small quarry exposing beds beneath the cornstones. These are the upper tilestones forming part of the original Silurian system (Sir R. Murchison). Fossil remains of fish and crustacea have been found, also flagstones covered with impressions of aquatic plants.

A special mention must be made of Hoarstone Farm (Hoarstone meaning boundary). This most important Grade II listed building is almost completely unaltered since medieval times. It is a Hall House of the 15th century containing two of the finest original Tudor fireplaces to be found in the country, each with beautifully carved oak lintels. One depicts figures in Tudor costume whilst figures of the first Red Indians to come to this country are elaborately carved out in the second lintel.

Park Attwood lies to the northern part of the parish of Trimpley, originating in a license granted in 1362 to John Attwood of Wolverley, the King's yeoman. In 1938 the estate was split up and sold. Later the Park Attwood became a hotel. During the Second World War the Royal Corp of Signals were billeted there. It is now a therapeutic centre where natural herbs and oils are used in the treatment of patients.

Trimpley reservoir and works were built to provide additional water for Birmingham. The banks of the reservoir were landscaped and planted with groups of trees to blend in with the valley of the river Severn. Large blocks of stone from the Forest of Dean were placed around the waters edge to give a natural appearance. The pumping of water from the river Severn into the reservoir commenced at the end of November, 1967.

Members of the public enjoy walking in the grounds of the reservoir and along the river bank situated within this scenic part of the Severn Valley. The Severn Valley Railway's steam trains pass by here en route from Bewdley to Bridgnorth.

Bite Farm is the home of Mr and Mrs Ken Briggs, 'Lord of the Manor'. Mr Briggs' late father, Mr J. J. Briggs purchased the Manorial Rights of commonland. Mrs Briggs is well known for her work involving the preservation of several rare species of goat. These include Pigmys (Equatorial Africa), Bagot, of which only one hundred are left and Golden Guernsey which almost became extinct during the German occupation of the Channel Islands. Mrs Briggs' work is to be commended in the preservation of these species for future generations.

Upper Welland ❧

At the turn of the century, Upper Welland was as thriving a small community as nearby Welland. Bread, cakes, groceries, meat, haberdashery, hats and even boots and shoes were sold in separate shops frequented by local people. 'Jenkin's fast Walkers' were known for miles around as the boots in the window of a tiny shop, tied in pairs by their laces.

Until the 1970s, two places of worship were supported by the village. The Church of the Good Shepherd, a Mission Church, is now a dwelling but its window is in the mother church. A Mr Chadney built the still thriving Methodist church in 1886 along with two houses further up the village. Benton House gave its name to the Close of recently built starter-homes. Local tradition has it that the owner was 'bent-on' building and what 'e'd do, e'd do!' – hence the name of the second house Edo Place. He certainly beautified the village with alternating laburnum and red hawthorn trees.

Upper Welland's origins lie in a group of smallholdings around Seat's Common which was all Assart's land, so called because it was cleared, by permission given to the Little Malvern monks, from virgin forest. Dating from 1730, the oldest surviving house was originally The Black Horse Inn whose one-time landlord, Joe Potter, had the doubtful reputation of being able to swear so loudly he could be heard at the top of the Malvern Hills.

The local house names Pitville and Sandford commemorate a useful claypit. Assarts Lane clearly shows the village beginnings and the local pub is now The Hawthorn.

Upton Snodsbury ❧

In a hamlet adjoining Upton Snodsbury lies Cowsden which has approximately 15 dwellings. In one Mr Alfred Stevens, known to all as Nimmy, lives.

In this day and age the village daily papers are delivered by car but not in the days when the paperman was Nimmy. Nimmy delivered papers on

167

a pushbike. Every day he would ride very early to collect the papers from Worcester and on his return deliver them to almost every house. This he did in all sorts of weather, sometimes having to push his bike, but he always made sure that one received a paper whatever time of day it was. In the 40 years that Nimmy was the paperman he provided a valuable service to the community.

Not very far from the high road which runs through Upton Snodsbury lies an old thatched cottage. It has a good piece of garden and windows high up under the eaves, and is still inhabited today. Few of the residents of today trouble to remember the terrible crime enacted there on a dark November night many years ago. On the night of November 7th 1707, Mrs Palmer and her maid, who lived here alone were murdered and the house partly burnt by a gang of desperate villains, at the head of whom was John Palmer, her son, and Thomas Symonds whose sister was Palmer's wife. The murderers were hanged in chains for their horrible crime and Hobbins and Allen, two others of the gang were also hanged.

Upton Warren ✿

Between Bromsgrove and Droitwich, Upton Warren lies sandwiched between the busy A38 and the M5 motorway. It is a small village with an ancient church serving a scattered rural parish.

By the A38 trunk road, the Worcestershire Nature Conservation Trust has created a haven of peace and quiet for a wide variety of birds which are attracted to the old flooded gravel workings, some of which are saline due to the proximity of the saltworks at Stoke Prior. An adjoining lake has been developed by the County Council as a dinghy sailing instruction centre for young people from all over the county.

Warndon ✿

To most people this name is now that of a large housing estate on the edge of Worcester. Prior to the 1950s it was a rural backwater and the little church of St Nicholas with its black and white timbered tower and interior of rustic simplicity, furnished throughout with shoulder high box pews, could only be reached by an unfenced, gated road through farm meadows leading into a farmyard whence led steep steps and a gravel path up to the church door.

168

Welland 🐏

What was it about Welland that made the family of gypsy travellers decide in the 1920s and 1930s to settle there? Perhaps to them it represented the typical English village with its wealth of agricultural work and convenient situation between Upton-on-Severn and Malvern.

Ishmail and Lilo James were so fond of the area that one day on walking from the Pheasant Inn, Ishmail tossed a stone over the church wall vowing that where it fell that is where he and his wife would be buried. This wish was carried out and the grave marked with a headstone can be seen there today.

Their two sons, Esau and Thomas, continued to live in their caravan beside a stream at the bottom of Garrett Bank. Neither could read nor write but each earned a good living working for local farmers. Ferrets which were fed on birds shot with a muzzle-loading gun were kept for rabbiting and being expert poachers they lived well. After their deaths when both were in their late 70s, their caravan and all possessions were burned to the ground by their surviving relatives.

In the late 19th and early 20th centuries Welland was widely known for its annual fete which was the only event of its kind for miles around. Older villagers remember that it nearly always rained but this did not deter crowds from coming from far and near. The event was held in a field behind the Pheasant Inn where sports and competitions were organised, including bowling for the pig, tug-o-war and a coconut shy. Other entertainments were roundabouts, swings, dodgems and numerous 'try your luck' stalls followed in the evening by dancing to live music in a marquee. The bar, open all day, did a roaring trade and weary competitors of the popular circular walking race of about 3 miles, particularly appreciated being able to quench their thirst.

In the two decades before the war apple orchards were abundant in the village and many farmers produced their own cider. Perhaps the best known were the Wastie family of Lawn Farm whose extensive orchards produced a cider of high quality winning many prizes at agricultural shows both in the Midlands and West Country.

It is not clear how the village acquired its name. One theory is that in pre-Norman Conquest days when the area was almost certainly dense forest, it was owned by a man called Wenna. Eventually, Wenna's land became known as Welland. After the Norman Conquest it was made a Royal Forest or Chase which meant that it was still thickly wooded and possibly discouraged settlement. Only in the 13th century is there mention of a chapel being built about 1½ miles east of the present centre of the village. Since then several churches have occupied this site but all that remains here today is an overgrown churchyard close to Welland Court, one of the oldest houses in the area.

Welland enjoys superb views of the changing moods of the 9 mile stretch of Malvern Hills, is dominated by the spired Victorian church of St James' and from its two housing estates, the most recent built in the 1970s, many inhabitants commute daily to various towns and cities.

West Malvern

West Malvern is far from being the typical English village. Instead of thatched cottages clustered gently around a green, the houses are perched, higgledy-piggledy, on the steep western slopes of the Malvern Hills. The main road follows the contour line, the side roads are precipitous and narrow. At this height, the very climate differs from surrounding areas, and they get more snow, more low cloud and earlier frosts. As recompense the villagers enjoy glorious views, and it is said that, on a clear day, from the top of the Worcester Beacon one can see a sixth of England and Wales.

The setting of West Malvern has determined its character and development from the start. In pre-Victorian times the usual country activities were varied by quarrying and lime kilns. During the 19th century, fired by the upsurge of interest in Malvern as a fashionable spa, several wealthy and prominent citizens made their homes here. They in turn attracted cultured and philanthropic friends and many substantial houses were built during that period, giving a new range of employment to local people.

The curious juxtaposition of the old-established local people, and their rural roots and folk memories of the old days, with the world-travelled, hill-walking newcomers produced a fascinating mixture. Happily, genuine, irreplaceable examples of both extremes are still to be seen, now very old, striding the Hills. Happily too, there is no polarisation, and, over the course of a century, retired nomads have found security in West Malvern, while the locals have had gusts of fresh air from the wide world outside with which to invigorate themselves.

In the 19th century West Malvern still had the Mummers' Play at Christmas, with whole passages of the script handed down orally from the 15th century. The young men of the village sewed fluttering patches of bright colours to their clothes and went from house to house with the play. On one occasion, carried away with the fire and zest of the performance, a participant, Mr Bethel, was knocked unconscious. Thereafter he was always known as 'Crack' Bethel, or 'Old Crack'.

A village landmark which has disappeared is The Redan Public House, named after a Russian stronghold in Sebastopol. Old photographs show it to be huge and barrack-like. It was built, at great expense, and on 'spec', by a local builder in the 1850s. The builder evidently had bitten off more than he could chew, for a creditor obtained a committal order for non-payment of debt. The Redan, though, was constructed like a fortress, and the builder immured himself there for 20 years, only emerging in the hours of darkness, when arrest for debt was not permitted. He eventually died there, and, until its demolition many years later, a ghost story persisted at the old pub. Even now, and probably for ever, the site is known as 'The Redan Bend'.

One could list endlessly the activities of the churches, the thriving current social activities, the clubs and societies, the neighbourliness, the friendships. But West Malvern's special flavour comes from contrasts and exists primarily because of its geographical location, which has given it the contrast of Victorian grandeur cheek by jowl with humble cottages; its world class girls school just across the road from the County Primary; its accessibility to the world for most of the year, and its total isolation during the snow, when the clock goes back 200 years at a stroke.

Whitbourne ✤

Whitbourne village came into being round the manor or palace of the Bishops of Hereford, as a community of the workpeople of the manor. The present church dates from 1180 but is probably built over the foundations of an earlier smaller church which was the chapel of the Bishop's palace. All the land round Bromyard, quite a large estate, had been given to the Church. The packhorse bridge over the brook, known as the 'Bishop's bridge', was built by an early bishop to enable visitors with pleas, and stores for the moated house, to arrive without crossing the ford. There was no other bridge in the village until late last century.

There are a number of half-timbered houses in the bottom lane dating from the 14th century. One was built as a hostel for travellers coming to see the bishop, where they could spend the night before seeing him after their long ride. This was later turned into an inn, but for a century or two has been a private house. The original inns were The Boat Inn on the river Teme which was demolished at the end of the last century, and the Live and Let Live, which is still in being, with a Victorian brick frontage. The Wheatsheaf Inn on the main road was built as a coaching inn in the days of the turnpike roads.

In the Civil War, the people of Whitbourne were staunchly Royalist, and with pitchforks and scythes tried to prevent a number of Roundheads from crossing the Teme to enter the village. However, the Roundheads had a cannon with them and won the day. The soldiers marched up Boat Lane and occupied the Bishop's palace. When the Boat Inn at the ford was demolished at the end of the last century, a cannon ball was found embedded in the walls.

At the end of the Commonwealth, the palace was partially demolished and the land bought by Col. Birch (who later became an M.P. in the county). He built the present Whitbourne Court over the gate-house of the old palace, filling in part of the moat to do so. In the 1970s the Court was turned into three houses.

The village had extended to Meadow Green at the top of the hill in the village, and with the end of the feudal days, farms had sprung up all over the parish. Meadow Green is now the village centre. It is a large parish, 16 miles in circumference, and the bounds were last beaten in the early 1930s.

In 1850 the school was built on Meadow Green, and in 1875 a second large classroom at right angles to the first, was added. This extended over the old lane, thus making the hair-pin bend in the middle of the village, now marked with plentiful yellow lines. The new classroom was used for concerts and village dances until after the First World War, when the Ex-Servicemen's Hut was put up on the land given by Capt E. F. H. Evans, whose family had built Whitbourne Hall in palatial style in the 1860s, and this served as a village hall until the present Coronation Hall was opened in 1963.

This has always been a go-ahead and friendly village, and now, with the population doubled in the last 15 years, there is no danger of losing the school, post office or rectory. The church parish has been widened to take in five neighbouring small villages and villagers feel all set for another eight centuries at least!

White Ladies Aston 🦜

The village was once known as Aston Episcopi Aston, being the settlement east of Worcester. 'White Ladies' were nuns of a Cistercian order based at Whitestone in the city, circa 1300. The church of St John the Baptist, with its weather-boarded bell-turret and spire, dates from Norman times and still has several features of that period.

Whittington 🦜

Whittington is a village on Worcester's south-eastern border, a green jewel in a concrete ring. Saxons settled its boundaries 1200 years ago and named it after their headman Whita. The Charter of AD 960 details those bounds and they still hold good, save for one corner nipped off by the city in 1931 and densely populated since then. The area left to Whittington Parish Council contains five farms and has about 400 inhabitants.

Whittington church was built in 1844 by A. E. Perkins in local stone in the place of a 15th-century half-timbered church which itself must have been a replacement, for back in the 10th century Whittington was one of the 11 chapels served by priests based on St Helen's, the first church in Worcester. The churchyard contains a yew tree whose girth proves it to have been planted in about 1270 and there would have been a churchyard before there was a church. Since 1985 Whittington has been a second parish in the ecclesiastical parish of St Martin's with Whittington.

The village's outstanding topographical feature is Crookbarrow Hill. Viewed from the A44 dual-carriageway, it rises sheer, with the half-moated Tudor Crookbarrow Farm house nestling against it. Its 6 acres, formerly fenced, are all grassland and part of the farm. Locally a far commoner name for it is Whittington Tump. Its likeness to the scriptural Calvary and to the hymn-writer's 'green hill far away without a city wall' led to a lot of Worcester families at the turn of the century walking out to Whittington Tump on Good Friday afternoon. The view from the top takes in Bredon Hill and the Malverns and more hills to the west. The last celebration bonfire there was in 1977 at the Queen's Silver Jubilee. For the Britons, Romans and Saxons in peace and war it was a key lookout post, and so in the Second World War it was for the Home Guard. There are those who want to explain it as man-made, but it is infinitely more

Crookbarrow Hill, known locally as Whittington Tump

likely to have been a natural deposit originally at the bottom of the inland Severn Sea, in which Bredon and the Malverns were islands.

Whittington's village school was started by the Church of England in 1858 and until 1919 took children up to the school-leaving age of 14. Under the 1944 Education Act its age range has been from 5 to 11. The site of the school is tucked away from traffic and next to a playing field of its own. The church is only ¼ mile away and school services there are crowded with children and parents. The school enriches the village and the village is proud of the school.

A newer post-war asset has been the village hall, opened in November 1954 and, as a result of frequent improvements, now provided with excellent car parks and kitchen facilities, a committee room and a new stage, with a good dance floor. In 1987 this hall won the County Best-Kept Village Hall Competition in the under-600 inhabitants' Class.

The Swan Inn supplies the community's remaining need. It is a three storey Georgian building and a popular resort for all sorts of adult customers from a 5 mile radius. When the Southern Link Road reaches the vicinity of the Swan and the Great St Peter development is complete, the Swan will be more accessible and hospitable still.

Wichenford 🌿

The parish of Wichenford lies in the fertile, heavy clay land between the rivers Severn and Teme, a feature which some say gives the area its own individual soft climate encouraging lush pastures for cattle and sheep as well as cereals, root crops and fruit trees. The land is well watered by two brooks feeding into the Teme to the south and another into the Severn to the north. Until the middle of this century the population, now numbering around 450, lived in rather secluded groups of small hamlets, scattered farmsteads and cottages. In 1953, however, a row of council houses, known because of the coronation as the Queen's Estate, was built which gave a new centre to the village. Since then several owner-occupied houses and bungalows have been added thus extending the size of Wichenford village considerably. As a consequence, apart from a few notable exceptions such as the Bakery, the Old Smithy, the School House and a few cottages, the village looks fairly new. A visitor could therefore be excused for thinking that little history attaches to the area.

Far from it! The land remained in the hands of the Church after the Norman Conquest, being given to the Church of Worcester by a grant of King Offa of Mercia sometime in the latter half of the 8th century. Nearly all the farms go back well over 200 years and many of the fields retain the names of pre-Saxon times such as Verm Meadow, Far Mallenders, Banky Orles, Lower Quarrell and Cuckoo Penn. The parish church of St Laurence was consecrated in November 1269, the oldest bell in the tower being dated between 1486–89, the two others being hung in 1664 and 1673. Records and drawings of the church made in 1825 show many differences to the present building. Extensive restoration was carried out in 1861–3 to remove what were considered to be 'tasteless alterations'. Perhaps sadly this included the removal of the minstrels gallery which in the early 19th century accommodated a little band playing the flute, violin and clarinet. This left the church as we now see it; an idyllic setting among rolling meadows.

The name Wichenford probably derives from 'ford by some wych elms'. This ford went through the Fitchers Brook which flows between the parish church and Wichenford Court. This latter is a large and imposing house whose Caroline exterior, built in 1710, conceals an Elizabethan structure which probably contained fragments of a larger medieval mansion. This was reputed to have been one of the largest in the county complete with moat and drawbridge.

In addition to the Court itself, in the grounds right on the edge of the road, a very attractive feature of Wichenford is a large barn measuring 160 feet by 78 feet constructed in 1697 of timber and wattle and originally thatched. Behind the barn is a rare 16th century dovecote in an unusually fine condition now maintained by the National Trust and open to visitors.

The Memorial Hall was built just after the First World War in memory of the ten men from Wichenford who lost their lives. In 1977 a Day Centre for the handicapped was set up but this moved from the Hall to some of the school buildings a few years ago when sadly the school was closed. Despite this and the loss of the incumbent vicar the village is thriving with its recent increase in population. Every year a very popular Church Fete is held in the grounds of the Court as well as other events such as an open day for SSAFA. Other activities include the usual country pursuits of hunting and shooting which continue to provide this little community with a sense of identity which is firmly rooted in the past and its traditions.

Wickhamford ✒

Just 2 miles from Evesham on the busy A44 to Broadway, lies Wickhamford, one of the most delightful and prettiest of all the villages in this fertile Vale of Evesham. Wickhamford is not only as old as Domesday, but even older! It was one of the settlements received by St Egwin from the Saxon King Offa in AD 703 as the founding endowment of Evesham Abbey. The name is derived from the Saxon tribe of Hwicca, the word 'hamm' meaning a bend in the river and 'ford' a place to cross the river.

The heart of the old village is set just off the main road, among trees, close to the Badsey Brook with its waters rushing over a small weir. Here are timber-framed farmhouses and age-old cottages, also the 16th century gabled and timbered Manor House and the small 13th century church of St John the Baptist.

The Manor House was built on the site of an earlier Grange belonging to Evesham Abbey and remained their property until the Dissolution of the Monasteries in 1539. In 1594 it was purchased by Sir Samuel Sandys, the eldest son of Edwyn, Archbishop of York and one-time Bishop of Worcester. The Manor and estates then remained in the Sandys family until 1868. In the beautiful landscaped gardens behind the Manor House are the remains of what was once a monastic fish-pond. Also still standing today (and inhabited) is a dovecote built by Abbot Randolf in 1214 to provide the monastic pigeon pie!

Next door to the Manor stands the church, a veritable treasure-house, containing many interesting features. Not least among these are the fine canopied alabaster monuments to the Sandys family, the three-decker pulpit (one of only a few remaining in this country), the beautiful carved panels on the box-pews and the floor-slab memorial to Penelope Washington. American visitors are particularly interested in this lady as she was the daughter of Colonel Henry Washington and a relative of George Washington.

Along Manor Road stands the Memorial Hall, the hub of many activities in the village. Here meet a flourishing Women's Institute, a Gardening Club, a Youth Club, a Friendship Club for the older members of the community and many more activities.

The well-kept cottage gardens of Wickhamford are a joy to behold, not only in the summer but in all seasons and villagers are proud of the fact that they have won the Best Kept Village Competition twice in recent years and also the Tidy Churchyard Competition. To commemorate this latter event a tree was planted in the churchyard by the present Lord Sandys.

Although only a small village Wickhamford has an industrial estate unobtrusively tucked away behind the plum trees on Pitchers Hill and on the other side of the main road are the kennels of the National Canine Defence League also blending inconspicuously into the landscape. In more recent years, since the decline of market gardening, the village has become renowned for its roadside stalls, where local growers ply their business with a very high standard of quality and service. One local entrepreneur even became famous for his large jars of pickled onions! On any busy summer's day touring coaches and cars can be seen drawn up off Pitchers Hill loading up with a supply of local asparagus, plums, apples, strawberries, or whatever is in season.

All told, one can safely say that although Wickhamford has a 'commercial' end and an 'olde worlde' end, there is an invisible bond between these two halves which fuses together to form one happy, lively and sociable community.

Wilden ❧

The village of Wilden is a compact little village situated for the most part on the side of a hill. It has the river Stour running on its western border and is not far from the mighty river Severn. There is a considerable amount of open space and the fields known as the Water Fields are now the property of the National Trust.

In former years it boasted an Ironworks, belonging to the Baldwin family. Now the site is a thriving industrial estate.

The generosity of the late Mr Alfred Baldwin (the father of Stanley Baldwin, who was at one time Prime Minister, and who later became the first Earl Baldwin of Bewdley), provided a magnificent little church and a very good First School. It always radiates happiness when one visits the school. One quaint custom of the school is remembering once a year an old farm labourer, Thomas Jones, who from his meagre wage of 12/6d per week, managed to leave a sum of money to provide a tea party for the youngsters. As a thank you on one particular day in July of each year the children place posies of flowers on his tombstone.

The church is a very compact building, and is the proud possessor of some really magnificent stained-glass windows, all designed by Sir Edward Burne-Jones. The magnificent east window was given by Mr and Mrs Alfred Baldwin as a thank offering for a happy married life. The church's Sanctuary curtains are unique in that they are perfect examples of Victorian church embroidery and the magnificent gold altar frontal worked by the Macdonald sisters is indeed famous, having been loaned out for several important exhibitions at The Victoria and Albert Museum.

There is a very well run village hall, which is kept in tip top condition and eminently suitable for meetings, wedding receptions etc, and a very successful Whist Drive is held there once a fortnight. There is also a well appointed Sports Club with plenty of playing space for cricket and football.

The village also boasts a large well-stocked fishing pool. This, however, belongs to the owners of the industrial estate and permission has to be sought to fish therein.

Wilden has a very well run village grocery shop and post office, and three pubs – The Wilden Inn, The Rock and The Bay Horse. It is well served with local farmers and coal merchants, and has a good half hourly bus service. All in all this little village is a very comfortable and happy place to live in.

Witton 🌿

This village's main claim to fame is that one of its sons became Governor of the colony of New Plymouth. The parish church of St Peter de Witton records the birth and baptism of Edward Winslow. He was educated at King's School, Worcester and apprenticed to a London printer. He sailed with the Pilgrim Fathers in 1620 to the New World.

Wolverley 🌿

Wolverley is a village situated at the confluence of the Horsebrook and river Stour on the northwest boundary of Worcestershire.

The principal features today include a canal completed by Brindley, Primary, Middle and Comprehensive schools, a private school, three residential homes for the elderly and two holiday caravan sites.

In the centre of the old village are the post office and delicatessen. There are four public houses, all of which provide food for the many visitors.

As a memorial to the men and women who fought and died in the wars, the villagers raised the money to erect the large Memorial Hall, in which many local functions take place. Adjoining this is the social club with extensive recreational facilities, tennis courts and a bowling green among them. In addition to these the village has a large playing field for football and cricket.

Overlooking the village, stands the church of St John the Baptist, in a commanding position on a hill.

Wolverley derives its name from that of Wulfeard the leader of a Saxon band, who in 866 was given land in this locality by Burgred, King of Mercia. The Charter recording this gift is still in existence, and is so clear in its detail that the members of the local history group were able to identify the landmarks named, and so walk round the old boundary.

The Legend of the Knight of Wolverley tells of Sir John Atewode (Attwood), who went to fight in a holy war against the Saracens and Pedro the Cruel, King of Castile. Having been imprisoned by Infidels, Sir John was released from his incarceration by an angel and was carried, on the back of a swan, to a field adjoining his home in Wolverley; this field bears the name of Knight's Meadow to this day. There he was found by a dairy maid, who failed to recognise him because of his emaciated condition. However, his faithful dog knew him at once. His lady, believing him to be dead, was about to remarry, but was reunited happily with her knight before the ceremony could take place.

In the church today, the broken effigy of the knight is on display and a set of fetters said to have been taken from Sir John are still to be seen in a house in the village.

'Inheritance by Borough English' was a practice kept here. This meant that the youngest child was heir to the father. This may be the reason why William Sebright, the eldest son of a prominent local farming family, went to London to seek his fortune, where he subsequently became a wealthy merchant and Lord Mayor. At his death in 1620, he left property in London, the income from which was to be devoted to the education of the children in Wolverley. A free grammar school was built in the village and from then on, with the London property appreciating in value, the village has profited by bequests from the Sebright Foundation.

Interesting features of the area are the complex cave dwellings which were developed by excavating the soft sandstone cliffs, during the Industrial Revolution. These were to provide living accommodation for workers in the iron factories. Some of these dwellings were still occupied as recently as 30 years ago.

The present day village has an electorate of 1700 and is becoming increasingly popular for retirement and for homes from which to commute to the industrial areas of the West Midlands.

Wood Norton

To most travellers on the B4084 out of Evesham, Wood Norton is the BBC Engineering Training Centre, with its modern buildings nestled incongruously in the hillside, overlooking the river Avon. To those who glimpse the magnificent double gates guarding one of the original entrances, there is an indication that there may be more to Wood Norton than simply an educational establishment for aspiring technicians. There, amongst the residential blocks and lecture rooms, stands Wood Norton House, once the home of the Duc d'Orleans.

At the turn of the century the owner of Wood Norton enjoyed a lifestyle that was beyond the imagination of his tenants down in Norton and Lenchwick, with its groups of half-timbered cottages and smallholdings.

The house was approached by two beautifully wooded, winding drives and those gates, which now hint of an opulent past, are said to have originally stood at the entrance to the Royal Palace of Versailles, and to have been valued at £15,000. Only Royalty were allowed to pass through the gates; other visitors had to use the less conspicuous entrance further down the road.

Perhaps one of the most interesting rooms in the house is the Duc's bathroom, which boasts several kinds of baths, the most impressive, surely, a sumptuous square one with four or five steps leading down and a series of taps to provide the ultimate in early 20th century bathing. No outside pump to fill the bath tub here!

At the rear of the house the Duc built a museum to accommodate treasures collected on his many expeditions – an elephant, complete with howdah and passengers, a replica of the cabin of a ship in which he journeyed, and the kennels of the dogs which accompanied his party, to remind him of his epic voyage to the Arctic.

The Duc also kept a private zoo, including wallabies, red deer, an emu, wild boars and bears. The bear pit was later to become a swimming pool and the bear houses, the dressing rooms.

Before the First World War, the Duc, apparently pressed by creditors, sold the estate and lived out the last years of his life on the island of Sicily – the end of an era for Wood Norton.

Wribbenhall & Bewdley

Wribbenhall and Bewdley are delightfully situated on the eastern and western side of the middle reaches of the river Severn and connected by the elegant stone balustraded bridge built by Thomas Telford in 1798.

Wribbenhall once included Bewdley as one parish and the present church there was built in 1879 after Wribbenhall had been constituted a separate parish. The old church was pulled down and a stone cross erected on the altar site which can be seen today surrounded by a peaceful little garden by the Craft Centre in Wribbenhall.

The quays on either side of the bridge are reminders of Bewdley's great days as a port and a trading centre since prehistoric times. The carriage of goods by water was comparatively cheap and many residents of Bewdley and Wribbenhall engaged in trade on the river, either as merchants, shipbuilders or boatmen. Goods were brought by packhorse or wagon from the Black Country, Midland industries and Shropshire coalfields to the quays to await transportation down river to Worcester, Gloucester and Bristol, and in the 18th century to the American colonies. Fortunes

Bewdley Bridge, built by Thomas Telford in 1798

were made from these trading ventures and many fine 17th and 18th century houses, which still stand in Wribbenhall and Bewdley, were built by merchants from profits from this trade. The importance as a port dwindled rapidly after the completion of the Staffordshire and Worcestershire Canal in 1772.

On the eastern side of the river is Blackstone Rock and the caves in the sandstone rock were used as a hermitage in medieval times. Later, it is said, they were hiding places for smugglers' contraband.

Bewdley derives its name from the Norman French 'beaulieu' meaning 'beautiful place'. The description is well deserved and since the 18th century the centre of Bewdley has changed very little, most of the buildings remain unaltered, making it, in the words of the architectural historian Nikolaus Pevsner 'the most perfect small Georgian town in Worcestershire'.

A wide number of crafts and industries were practised in the area from the 16th century onwards. Brass and pewter were manufactured, and there is still a lane in Wribbenhall called Pewterer's Alley. Lowe's Rope Manufactory was established in 1801 in Wribbenhall and continued to make rope there until 1972.

Bewdley's museum is housed in The Shambles, a late 18th century market with a cobbled street flanked by arcades at the rear. The museum, opened to the public in 1972, contains many reminders of the days when Bewdley was one of Britain's most prosperous inland ports.

In recent years Wribbenhall's Junior School, built in 1850, has been converted to a Craft Centre for local people to demonstrate, show and sell their crafts to the public. The studios are open on most days and a tea room provides home-made refreshments for the visitors.

The Severn Valley Steam Railway, Safari Wild Life Park, museums and craft workshops attract many visitors to the area each year, and others come to admire the splendid old buildings or just to enjoy a pleasant walk by the river.

Wychbold ✤

The village of Wychbold lies on either side of the A38, midway between Droitwich and Bromsgrove. Wychbold is associated in many ways with the neighbouring villages of Upton Warren, Stoke Prior, Stoke Works, Stoke Heath and Stoke Pound – all mainly rural areas and so predominantly farming country, but there are also several industrial firms which give employment to many of the inhabitants.

The two 700 foot high masts of the BBC transmitting station at Wychbold were completed in 1934 and are a dominant feature of the Worcestershire landscape – many a homecoming traveller has been happy and relieved to see those familiar towering becons signifying the end of the journey.

Wychbold owes a tremendous debt to John Corbett, who transformed the working conditions at Stoke Prior Salt Works in the 1860s and developed the most efficient method of salt production in Britain. He built model housing for his employees, a school, a dispensary, almshouses for retired salt workers. He provided money and land for the building of St Mary de Wyche Church and Vicarage at Wychbold – completed in 1888. The church is built on a salt seam which has caused a certain amount of subsidence, evidenced by its leaning church tower and a pronounced and sometimes disconcerting slope to the floor in the main aisle.

John Corbett's selfless and Christian way of life did not ensure for himself a happy family life. He had married a well-born Irish lady in Paris in 1856 and they made their first home at Stoke Grange, (now Avoncroft College), Stoke Heath. Then in 1875 he built at Impney, between Rashwood and Droitwich, a chateau in the style of Louis XIII to please his wife who had been used to living in great style in France. This building was sited in 200 acres of parkland, providing a spectacularly beautiful and romantic sight, but sadly the marriage continued to deteriorate and ended in separation in 1884, when Mrs Corbett and their six children moved permanently to their second home by the sea in Wales. She is buried at Towyn and John Corbett, the 'Salt King', as he was known, died at Impney in 1901 and is buried at Stoke Prior.

Wychbold Hall, former home of the Amphletts, has an interesting history. There have been two Halls – the first was originally an old farmhouse bought by the grandfather of Judge Amphlett in 1825 but was demolished in 1936 owing to subsidence which had caused structural damage. A second Hall was built on a concrete raft some distance from the first residence and was a very fine mansion standing in wooded parkland. The Hall remained in occupation of the Amphlett family until 1955.

Rashwood Court was built in 1907 for Mr W. L. Hodgkinson, a respected member of the Catholic community and founder of the Sacred Heart Church at Droitwich. It is now a Residential Home for the Elderly.

The Crown Inn bears a date of 1728. It was modernised and major reconstruction work carried out in 1912. A remembered feature was a heated, salt-water swimming pool, the water being delivered by road tanker from Netherwich Pit, Droitwich.

The Brook House in Crown Lane bears on its wall a plaque which reads: 'The Most Reverend Edward W. Benson, D.D., Archbishop of Canterbury, when a boy, lived in this house with his father. The Archbishop died at Harwarden Castle on 11th October 1896, aged 67, when on a visit to the Right Honourable W. E. Gladstone, M.P.'

One of the oldest black and white farmhouses in the village is Astwood Manor Farm, parts of which were built in 1600. The Vicarage at Wychbold was built on land given by John Corbett, who also met part of the building costs.

During the Second World War, on 12th March 1941, a German Junkers 88, on an air-raid over Mersey-side, had been crippled by anti-aircraft fire. The pilot, before baling out with his crew, had set the plane on automatic course for eventual ditching in the North Sea, but the damage to its structure resulted in the aircraft moving in an arc which ended in a crash in front of 'The Croft'.

The nearby canal provides facilities for narrow boats, fishing and walking along the peaceful banks.

Wyre Piddle 🐚

Wyre Piddle lies on the elevated north bank of the river Avon about midway between Evesham and Worcester. In the centre of the village at the junction of Church Street with the Worcester Road stands the ancient preaching cross.

It is a chapelry in the parish of Fladbury. The major restoration of its small church 100 years ago revealed evidence that the site upon which it was built on the north bank of the river was well known as a burial place in pre-Christian times. The Anglo-Saxon artifacts discovered during the restoration are displayed in the church. The present building dates from the early Norman period, probably the first two decades of the 12th century.

Wyre was for centuries a quiet village community made up mainly of farming families, market gardeners, tradesmen and craftsmen whose work brought them to the village. No squire or parson dwelt amongst them. They occupied the timber-framed houses and thatched cottages on the river bank.

The opening up of the Avon navigation by William Sandys in the years 1636–1640 brought prosperity to the small village community. Two inns served the needs of the bargemen. The Anchor Inn, situated on the river bank continues to prosper and is one of the most popular inns on the Avon. The George Inn is now a private residence.

The march of time brought an alternative means of transport to Wyre which helped to contribute to the decline of river trade in the 19th century. The Oxford–Worcester–Wolverhampton railway line which ran through the village was finally opened in 1853. So many troubles bedevilled its development it became known as 'The old Worse and Worse'.

The village school was opened in the 1860s on land given for the building to the south of the church by Mr James Wagstaff of Wyre

House. The closure of Wyre School took place in 1958, an occasion of great sadness to many of the villagers.

The 1960s brought changes to Wyre far greater than any experienced throughout its history. The sale of Yew Tree farm in Church Street for the building of Avon Green, a development of 30 houses nearly doubled the population which had remained static at about 240 for 200 years or more. The influx of new residents on such a large scale broke down the old community and changed the character of the village in a single decade.

Many of the older villagers regret the passing of the old way of life and the neighbourliness and companionship it fostered. No longer are their lives centred around village institutions. Old customs have died – the Wyre Wake, the annual autumn fair, Maypole dancing in the village street, the Bretforton brass band which used to play around the village cross on Saturday evenings, and the processions to commemorate national events. There are no farmers in the village now. Only one market gardener carries on the traditional occupation.

In spite of the many changes however, or because of them, Wyre is still very much alive. The bakery shop, started 100 years ago, is still selling home made bread, and the village still has its post office.

Leisure and sport were revitalised in the village following the successful running of the Jubilee celebrations in 1977. The 100 Club was established and succeeded in raising £1000 towards the extension of the village hall, built in 1911 from money raised by a grand fete held in 1910. The well-maintained hall was entered in the Best Kept Village Hall Competition and tied for first place in 1984.

Wythall 🌿

Wythall is known as a village without a centre. It straddles the A435 in Worcestershire and has grown to a population of 12,500. The river Cole is its south-east boundary.

Wythall had a chapel in 1622 when Richard Moore had a licence to preach from his own home to people outside through a hole in the wall of a room called the curate's chamber.

By the early 18th century the roof of Wythall chapel was said to need repairing and in 1777 the chapel was being rebuilt. In 1826 the new building was described as a small brick building with a wooden bell turret and 29 pews. There was a school for 20 children by subscription and the desks were placed between the pews but removed for services.

The parish of Wythall was set up in 1853 (population approximately 1,000). In 1860 the churchyard was opened. Burials had previously been at Kings Norton with coffins being carried by bearers. Boys had carried stools so that the coffins could be rested on them on the way. A new church to seat 352 people was finished in 1862.

A school for 45 children was opened in 1841 near Wythall chapel (3 scholars) but by 1892 was extended to accommodate 14 more. This was used as St Mary's school until 1967, when Meadow Green infants and primary school opened. The old building became the Old School Hall to be used as a meeting place for church and other organisations.

From medieval times, the tanning industry was important in Wythall and there was a settlement and watermill at Tanner's Green. The industry flourished in the 17th and 18th centuries, possibly even as early as the 13th century. Withies grew in the area and were used for basket making.

There is little evidence now of the forests which once covered the area. The trees are predominantly English oak. Much of the land is used for grazing or sports fields and there are allotment areas.

Wythall Community Association purchased Wythall House in Silver Street in 1965 and provides sports and social facilities for 600 members. Wythall Institute was built in 1889, first used as a reading room, then as a hall for entertainment.

During the Second World War the RAF station opened in 1939 as a barrage balloon centre, became a training school for wireless operators and interpreters. Yew Tree Farm was demolished to create the airfield (now a new car depot).

Present day employment is limited, which results in 85% of residents being employed outside the area. Wythall relates in this way to Birmingham and to Bromsgrove District. There is a good road system linking Redditch with Wythall and Birmingham. Proximity to the M42 (and the proposed M40) increases community possibilities, making it a desirable residential area.

Shops, library, health centre, small businesses such as builders, schools and homes for the elderly provide jobs, and a farm shop draws customers from outside the area.

Wythall still holds its appeal for residents. Although the village has no centre it maintains its village atmosphere.

The village of Oddingley

Index